Unforeseen Tendencies
of Democracy

BY

EDWIN L. GODKIN, M. A., D. C. L.

BOSTON AND NEW YORK
HOUGHTON MIFFLIN COMPANY
The Riverside Press Cambridge

CONTENTS

INTRODUCTION

I HAVE endeavored in the following pages, not to describe democracy, — something which has been done by abler hands than mine, — but to describe some of the departures it has made from the ways which its earlier promoters expected it to follow. It has done a great many things which they never thought it would do, and has left undone a great many things which they thought it would do. Not nearly all the deductions from the principle of equality have been correct. The growth of democracy has dissipated a good many fears about the "mob;" but on the other hand it has failed to realize a good many expectations about its conduct of government. Nearly all the philosophers, from Tocqueville down, and especially the English Radicals of the earlier part of the century, would be surprised by some of its developments. No democratic state comes anywhere near their ideal. Unexpected desires and prejudices have revealed themselves.

Democracies have discovered new ways of doing things, and have discarded many old ones. More particularly they have not shown that desire to employ leading men in the management of their affairs which they were expected to show. In fact, that wish of the people to control their own business, which tormented the Old World for so many centuries, has been fully gratified, but the people are not managing them in the ways that were expected. Nearly all the recent writers on democracy, however, have assumed an inability on its part to correct mistakes, which the facts do not seem to me to warrant. Had it no such ability, the future of the world would indeed be pretty dismal. On the other hand, the error of its friends in defending it lies, it seems to me, in underestimating the length of time it takes a democratic community to find out that it is going wrong and to acknowledge it. It must be admitted, even by its warmest admirers, that democracy is not very teachable by philosophers and jurists. Experience counts with it for less than it used to count for, under the old aristocratic governments, but the reason seems to be that the experience of one class is seldom of much use to another. Each is apt to think it will do better by doing differently. Every democracy, too, is weighted by the fact that its new agents are rarely men familiar with public affairs, or with human trials in matters of government. Those of its advisers who are familiar with such things are apt to be hostile or distrustful, and are therefore not listened to with confidence or attention. It is, in fact, launched on a chartless sea, and most of its legislation hitherto has been mere groping.

The first danger it has encountered is the enormously increased facility for money-making which the modern world has supplied, and the inevitably resulting corruption. I cannot help doubting whether any régime would have withstood this. The power of getting money easily, debauched every court and aristocracy in the Old World, even when getting money easily meant mere rapine. The demoralization this is producing now, even among the scions of old houses, is one of the wonders of our time. Neither philosophy nor religion seems to offer much resistance to it. It is breaking down, not simply the old political, but the old social usages and standards. The aristocratic contempt for money as compared with station and honor, of which we used to hear so much, has completely vanished. The thirst for gold seems to be felt now by all classes equally, while the number of those among whom the gold has to be divided, is greatly increased.

Another disadvantage with which democracy has to contend, is being called on, almost suddenly, to govern the large masses of population called cities, without any experience, either of their special wants or of the means of satisfying them.

Our civilization has, as has been said, become urban within the present generation, almost without our knowing it. Democracy has therefore been suddenly called on to solve problems by universal suffrage which an oligarchy of the most select kind has never had to face. Its failures, therefore, have been serious and numerous, and there does not seem much chance of its doing better without experience; experience is a master from whose chastening rod none can escape. To suppose it will not learn through mishaps and miscarriages would be to despair of the human race, for it is from suffering or failure that we have got most of the good things in civilization. The great, perhaps the only, mistake optimists appear to make is, as I have said, the mistake of thinking there are short cuts to political happiness.

E. L. G.

UNFORESEEN TENDENCIES OF DEMOCRACY

FORMER DEMOCRACIES

I HAVE thought it necessary, at the risk of being tedious, to preface what I am about to say concerning democracy by a brief account of the earlier efforts to establish it. I do this to avoid the notion, which is only too prevalent, that we are in this age attempting something new in the art of government, when the fact is that we are continuing a very old experiment under widely changed conditions. Human nature remains the constant element in our problem, but it is now surrounded with a great variety of novel agencies, to which we are slowly and painfully trying to adapt ourselves.

There is probably no political question which has been more debated than the origin of society, — what it was that in the beginning brought large bodies of men together under one government. There is probably no subject more obscure.

When it began to be looked into after the Renaissance, the view of Aristotle, that society had grown naturally, was the one generally adopted. Government was the product of the nature of man as a gregarious or political animal, as he calls him. Men loved to live in a herd, and in order to live comfortably in a herd, regulations were necessary; and as soon as speech came, these regulations became governments, but they were not at the outset really what we call government. They were, more properly, customs. There is nothing more wonderful or incredible in these than in the customs of the bees or of the ants. These animals have certain ways of acting under certain circumstances, which must be considered, as long as we deny them intellect, a true government. That is, a certain course of conduct is imposed on them by some power or influence superior to the individual will. Whether this power be instinct or custom makes little difference. It constitutes an orderly way of living in society. The essential thing in any government is that it should make living in society easy and secure, while living alone is insecure and disagreeable. The prevalence of the belief among individuals that things must be done in a certain way, and not in others, and that unless things are done in a certain way, and not in others, unpleasant results will follow, means organized society; and it makes no difference from what source the unpleasantness of these results may emanate. As soon as this power or influence takes hold of men, and a number of them agree in submitting to it, government of some kind is instituted.

Of the origin of custom we know little, although there has been a great deal of speculation about it, too. But it is almost certain that every custom originated either in a common sense of the convenience of some practice, or in a gradually formed common belief in its efficacy as a protection against known ills. So it may be alleged with tolerable positiveness that the practice of being bound by certain customs was in the beginning a natural product of men's gregariousness.

A great deal, also, has been written about the origin of law. In the beginning of this century Austin made some impression by the definition of law as a command promulgated by an official superior; that is, he thought that there must be a government, in our sense of the word, before there is law, and that even custom does not become law until it has received the sanction or affirmation of this political superior, or of its courts or judges. But, as has been pointed out by Maine and Holland and Pollock, the courts decide what customs are binding and what are not, showing that a custom may be a law before the political superior takes any notice of it. In fact, it is now generally recognized, as Maine suggests, that law begins in custom or religion; that law is the product either of custom or of belief. As far as we can go back into the mists of time, we find men living under the domain of custom. We find them doing some things and avoiding others, simply because their fathers before them have done them or have avoided them. We find this long before we can catch sight of any political authority whatever. Even to-day, according to Mr. Lumholst, there are Australian savages who have no political or social superiors, and whom nobody commands. But they have rules of living. Superiority of physical strength seems to lead, in process of time, to the predominance of one man, which predominance finally brings with it moral influence. But political authority, apparently, does not come for a good while. Among American Indians, the chief is not always a political superior. He leads in a war party those who choose to follow him from confidence in his ability, but when the expedition is over he becomes simply a distinguished man, whose advice is valuable and whose prowess is great. What holds the tribe together is a collection of customs which fix the date and character of its doings, and which none dares to disobey.

Not unnaturally, when a chief of more than ordinary force and character is able, in a more advanced state of society, to convert this influence into positive rule, — that is, to make himself a Homeric or Roman "king," and perhaps a hereditary king, — to become a real political chief, and to give his family a semi-sacred character in the popular eyes, we have the foundation of a state.

But we meet with no sign in antiquity of the conscious foundation of a state by agreement. In all that we see or know of the foundations of society, we find no trace of conscious organization. Certain arrangements grow out of existing conditions. They are not made, and they differ infinitely as the previous circumstances differ. So that the Aristotelian view appears to have been founded on all that was known or could be learnt of the early history of mankind. The contract theory represented society as we see it, as having been founded by discussion between rulers and people, and the formation by mutual agreement of rules by which the government was to be carried on. This was, in the seventeenth century, the chief weapon of the friends of constitutional liberty against the absolutists. Sir Robert Filmer, on behalf of the absolutists, founded the monarch's claim to rule on the paternal character of Adam. As Adam

ruled all that then existed of the human race in
virtue of his fathership, so the kings ruled his
descendants as his successors, in virtue of their
fathership. Grotius went halfway towards this
theory by founding the monarch's title, not on a
contract with the governed, but on the consent
of the governed. They gave themselves to the
monarch without conditions. Hobbes held that
men formed society through fear of each other:
each, being afraid the others would kill or rob
him, thought it best for safety to enter into
an alliance with somebody, and thus tribes, and
finally societies, grew up. But all agreed that
in the original state of nature men lived as individuals, without relations with other men. Grotius made his theory support the existing condition of things on the continent of Europe. Sir
Robert Filmer used his to defend the cause of
King James, and Hobbes his to exalt the power
of "the state," or "Leviathan," in behalf of
King Charles. Hooker, as a moralist, used his
theory to inculcate the duty and advantages of
mutual love and assistance, whatever the form
of government might be. Locke held to the
contract theory on behalf of King William; but
the only government he could have known to
result, as Hooker says, from "the deliberate
advice, consultation, and composition between
men," was that of the New England colonies,

and more particularly that of Plymouth. What happened in "the state of nature," though described by nearly all these writers with minuteness, is pure guesswork.

Although Locke and Hooker described a free commonwealth or a "perfect democracy" with tolerable accuracy as the "majority making laws for the community from time to time, and executing those laws by officers of their own appointment," we really get no glimpses of a "people" as we understand the word in the modern world. A people, in the political sense, has to be not simply a collection of individuals or families living in a certain region in a certain way, and making common cause against enemies, but a body conscious of its own existence as a political organism, and of the existence of certain duties of individuals to one another without blood relationship, and of rights of its own, and of control over its own affairs as a whole, and of the power to dispose of itself as a whole. When this self-consciousness first arose we do not know. We find all writers on government, down to the French Revolution, treating the states of antiquity, and especially the Hebrews, Greeks, and Romans, as illustrations or proofs of their theories. What was right politically was generally found in the Bible; what was wise or admirable was generally found in Plu-

tarch's Lives or in Livy. Indeed, it may be said
that before Montesquieu there was no political
speculation worth serious attention. He was the
first since Aristotle to base his theories on the
nature of man, and to some extent on the experience of existing states. As he says in his preface, "I have not drawn my principles from my
prejudices, but from the nature of things." He
was, in fact, the first to consider the effects of
character on government, and to look on government as modifying character. But he continued, like his predecessors, to find most of his
illustrations in antiquity. This gave much of
the writing on politics of the pre-Revolutionary
period an academic air. Even Rousseau and
Voltaire and the Encyclopædists seemed to be
making literature rather than exerting an influence on government. It was not until the Revolution had sought to embody these speculations
in practice that democracy, or the rule of the
people, came out of the closets of the philosophers, either as a beneficent force or as a new
kind of danger, and that discussions about government took on an air of real business. The
Revolution sought to embody the speculations of
the philosophers in practice, not so much because
it fancied their theories as because the nation
was miserable. Had the French people been
happy and prosperous, or well governed, the

probabilities are that we should have heard little or nothing of the influence of the writers.

There is no doubt that the pre-Revolutionary writers were in the right way in relying on Greece and Rome for their illustrations. Up to that time the modern world, if we except England, had contributed little or nothing to the science of government. Certain customary bodies had grown up, such as the States-General in France and the House of Commons in England, which kept alive the theory that the people had something to do with the management of their own affairs. But as a rule government was in all countries a congeries of customs, maxims, or proverbs, literally without form and inexplicable, for which little could be said except that they had grown up, and that people were used to them and liked them. Symmetry was the last thing they sought. The ignorance and barbarism of the Middle Ages lingered in the laws and governmental arrangements of every European country. To get an idea of the orderly growth of states, as the result of manners, circumstances, and religion, readers have to go back to Greece and Rome.

Greece and Rome are, in truth, our political ancestors. From them have come to us, through some process of descent, the idea of nearly all our political arrangements. The habit

of taking counsel together is a natural result of
man's gregariousness.   But the practice of persuasion by discussion, and decision by a majority after a hearing, is Greek.   The use of checks
in the exercise of authority by law, and indeed
the habit of trying experiments in politics, are
Greek and Roman.   The Greeks and Romans
were the first we know of to make special machinery of government, to see how it would
work, and to change it deliberately if it was
unsuitable.   The Greeks may be said to have
been the founders of what is called " diplomacy ; " that is, of the art of conducting negotiations and transacting business through argument between equal states.   The Romans set us
the example of basing political arrangements on
manners and religion.   They took the family as
their political model, and created the political
father called the " king," or leader ; but they
kept in mind that as there were many fathers,
there must be discussion and agreement.   They
were the first, too, to embody in their polity a
full recognition of the value of experience and
deliberation by creating a body of seniors, or
older men, called the " Senate."   The early Roman Senate was composed simply of older men.
To compose it mainly of distinguished public
servants was the idea of a much later period.

In fact, what strikes one most, in reading the

history of either ancient Greece or Rome, is its
political activity, the incessantness with which
the people sought after better ways of living in
society. Greece was, for this purpose, somewhat in our position ; that is, it was made up
of a number of small states, in which constant
experimentation in politics was going on, within
limits set by a certain number of Hellenic customs which roughly corresponded to our Federal Constitution. Every one of the small states
tried something new, — monarchy, democracy,
or aristocracy, military or peaceful habits, — and
accepted or rejected it after trial. What is in
our eyes most singular in these trials is the part
distinguished men played in them. In nothing
political do we differ more from the ancient
world than in the disappearance from among
us of the "lawgiver," Moses, Solon, Lycurgus,
Minos, — the single statesman to whom the
people commit the construction of a social and
political régime by which they agree to live, or at
least to try to live. We can hardly conceive of
a state of mind in which we should be willing to
leave to one man, however revered, the construction of a plan of life both civil and political, —
sometimes, as in the case of Sparta, of great
severity, — and then accept it, without question,
for an indefinite period. According to Plutarch,
the Spartans lived for five hundred years under

laws of extraordinary rigidity contrived by Lycurgus. Solon at Athens, too, appears to have
had no difficulty in enforcing the *seisachtheia*,
or general release of debtors, in order to make
way for his code of laws, and Moses, or some
one of somewhat similar authority, supplied the
Hebrews with a moral code of the most endur-
ing character. It is to be observed, however,
that the lawgiver always acted with the aid of
religion. He was always supposed to have God
or his oracles behind him; that is, he had to be
in some sense divinely appointed. There is more
or less uncertainty about the exact nature of the
kind of legislation which each provided, but
no matter how mythical his character or doings
might be, the mere conception of the lawgiver
indicates a readiness to defer to individual wisdom, which has long departed from the world,
— the most remarkable feature of ancient politics.

But what was really almost as striking was
the capacity for general political progress of the
communities which sprang up in the numerous
islands and valleys of Greece, and of the various villages of shepherds and husbandmen who
founded Rome. We can hardly imagine similar
communities in our day doing more than live by
a small set of customs, tending their flocks, cul-
tivating their small farms, and only too happy

to walk quietly and unostentatiously in their
ancient ways.   The Greeks and Romans, on the
contrary, were remarkable for continuous search
after better ways.   The village on the Palatine
grew into an empire through a series of experiments in war and peace.   There were constant
changes in the structure of the government from
Romulus down to Augustus, to meet some existing ill.   In like manner, every little community
in Greece was occupied in steady pursuit of a
better régime than that which it had.   As a
rule, each was a little democracy, engaged more
or less frequently in resisting the attempts of
rich men to set up either a monarchy or an
aristocracy.   These attempts were often successful for a time, but never permanently successful.
Down to the end, in spite of their early respect
for family, the Greeks appear to have remained
thoroughly democratic in their ideas and manners.   But the rich class were rarely content
with the existing state of things, always felt they
could do better if they had their way, and were
as purely selfish as aristocracies are apt to be.
They were convinced that the most important
interest of the state was that they, not the
many, should be happy and content.   Aristotle
furnishes several illustrations of this, the most
remarkable being the oath which he says was
taken by some of the oligarchies: "I will be

evil-minded towards the people, and bring on them by my counsel whatever mischief I can."

In Aristotle's "Politics," in fact, may be found the best thought of the ancient world about politics, and, in general, about life in an organized state. It is somewhat startling to see how small is the advance we have made on his ideas. That the great end of men in society should be, not simply to live, but to live well; that a free state should be composed of freemen; that a state in which the good of the rulers is sought rather than that of the many, is not a free state; that private property is essential; that no man is a citizen who does not share in the government; that a good citizen and a good man are synonymous terms; that no man should be judge in his own cause; that government should be adapted to the mental and moral condition of the governed; that every class in a state, if it gets possession of the government, is apt to seek its own advantage exclusively, — these are principles which have not been improved upon, and lie at the basis of all modern political constitutions.

The only matters on which we should be disposed, in modern life, to dissent from Aristotle are the judiciary and slavery. Judges, he thinks, in a democracy, should be numerous and elective, and he recognizes slavery as ordained by nature. But his description of the internal dangers of a state, of the different kinds of government which have been tried, of the objections to each, and of the things necessary to the successful practice of either monarchy, oligarchy, or democracy, has hardly been surpassed in our day, even with our vastly longer experience. From him we get the Greek idea of citizenship without qualification; that is, government by universal suffrage, without regard to rank or property. But this has to be received with some allowance, owing to the existence of slavery. In every Greek republic the laboring class were slaves and were excluded from all share in the government, so that we cannot say that any one state made the experiment of democracy, in the sense in which we understand it. Even in the successful democracies, the voters or citizens were, in a certain degree, an oligarchy, were possessed of property and independence, and had ample time to occupy themselves with politics and to go to the assemblies, or, as we say, "to attend to their political duties."

This points to other important differences between our idea of democracy and that of the ancients. With Aristotle, smallness was an essential condition of democracy. It was considered desirable that no democracy should be so large that all the citizens could not attend the general

assembly and take a personal part in legislating
and judging; also, that all citizens should be in
some measure known to one another and to the
magistrates. As the representative system had
not been invented, our plan of committing the
work of government to a class, while the rest of
the population give the bulk of their time to
some sort of bread-earning, was not known to
the ancients as democracy. Such a state of
things was not in their eyes a democracy, but an
oligarchy or a monarchy. The personal participation of the citizen in all deliberations was
essential. To secure this, as democracies grew
larger, and the poor found presence at the meetings of the assembly a hardship, they were paid
a small sum for their attendance, like our jurymen. Moreover, for the same reasons, every
democracy was supposed to consist of a city simply, with all citizens living within easy reach of
the agora or forum. Strangers and sojourners
and slaves, however numerous, were excluded
from citizenship, so that at Athens and Rome,
in the later days, the real citizens were in a small
minority, constituting what the French call the
pays légal; that is, the city or country recognized by or known to the law. This presence of
a body of persons sharing the life and interests
of the place, but not allowed to share in its government, was transmitted to the modern world,

and became a feature in all the municipalities of the Middle Ages, and even of the democratic cantons of Switzerland. The citizens or burgesses owned the state or city as property, and transmitted it to their children. They gave nothing to the non-citizens but permission to reside and protection. The idea that mere birth and residence ought to give citizenship gained ground only after the French Revolution, and was really not received in England until the reform of the municipalities in 1832. The old confinement of the citizenship to a small body of property-holders, or descendants of property-holders, undoubtedly gave the property qualification to such of the modern European states as set up an elected legislature or council. Down to the passage of the Reform Bill in England, the exclusion of all but freeholders from the franchise seemed a perfectly natural arrangement. It was very difficult for most Englishmen, and the same thing is true of the earlier Americans, to suppose that any one could take a genuine interest in the welfare of the country, or be willing to make sacrifices for its sake, who did not own land in it. The central idea of the ancient city was in this way made to cover the larger area of a modern kingdom.

This idea of citizenship, too, accounts in some measure for the important place assigned in the

Greek system to the "demagogue." Not only the name, but the picture of the demagogue comes to us from antiquity. He is literally a man who exerts great influence over the people, it may be for good as well as for bad purposes. We use the word in a bad sense, but originally the sense was not always bad. The demagogue was distinctly the product of oratory. It was oratory at Athens, for instance, which is said to have created him; and of course, to give weight to oratory, the body to be influenced must be small. To employ the common expression of our orators, those whom he addresses must be "within the sound of his voice." In the absence of a periodical press this was essential. The people must have been a body which a man could address even in the open air. His distinguishing trait, however, as Aristotle describes him, was his correspondence to the flatterer or courtier of the monarch or tyrant. He always extolled the wisdom and other good qualities of the people, and claimed in virtue of this wisdom very great powers for it. He was the great enemy of checks and balances. Aristotle describes one sort of democratic government as "allowing the people, not the law, to be supreme." "And this takes place," he says, "when everything is determined by a majority of voters, and not by a law, — a thing which happens by reason of the demagogues." They might, in fact, be described as the great champions, on every occasion, of government by simple majority, a characteristic which they possess in our day. Most demagogues maintain the wisdom of the people, not generally, but with regard to the particular matter under consideration; this wisdom is superior to all experience, to all checks imposed by antecedent laws or constitutions, and even to the moral ideas of any preceding generation. Their audience is always treated as either omnipotent or allwise within the sphere of legislation, and as much wronged by the restriction of its powers by any outward influence.

It is the remembrance of this fact which has led, in modern times, to the adoption of constitutions changeable only at fixed times or in a prescribed way. The main object of them all is to put restrictions on the power of the majority vote, which vote is an object of great dread to nearly all political philosophers in our day. On the other hand, the object of nearly all demagogues, as they are called, is to establish this power. This has perhaps never been more remarkably illustrated than by the recent presidential canvass in this country. All, or nearly all, Mr. Bryan's adherents wished, with regard to the currency and various other matters, to disregard the experience of the race and of the rest of the world, and to treat the wishes of the majority as sufficient to determine finally the action which the nation ought to take. This caution due to the fear of external resistance, which in previous democracies has generally been operative, was notably absent, owing to the unprecedented size of the democracy. The demagogues said that we were so large and powerful that we could do what we pleased. No ancient democracy was able to say this or think it. It always had neighbors of nearly equal strength, whose enmity was to be feared or whose good will had to be courted. What other neighboring states thought, or would be likely to think, of most measures under discussion, was generally a consideration of more or less weight. Then, the possibility of emigration on the part of any class or set of men whom legislation might oppress or discriminate against, had to be taken into account. The ancient world along the shores of the Mediterranean was constantly agitated by movements of discontented people in search of new homes. Seneca's explanation of the causes of the foundation of colonies would apply almost exactly to the seventeenth and eighteenth centuries. It would apply even to the emigration of this century, — with this difference, however : that the ancient colonists never went very far away, but settled in what might be called Greek or Roman regions, while ours, as a rule, have planted themselves in the wilderness, where the work of civilization had to be begun from the very foundations. The Swiss, from the earliest times, enjoyed this advantage of having powerful neighbors, whose presence exerted a more or less moderating influence on all democratic schemes or enterprises. Even their extraordinary military success in the sixteenth century did not rid them of the fear of foreign critics.

In all ancient democracies, including early Rome under this term, the internal history is generally an account of contests between the poor and the rich ; meaning by " poor " persons who are not rich, — not the extremely poor. An oligarchy always consists of rich men ; a democracy, of what may be called people of moderate means. For the most part, the rich seem never to be thoroughly content with the rule of the many, and long to rid themselves of it. Nor do they share the democratic or Aristotelian idea of the state as a community of freemen. They think themselves entitled to rule, and think their contentment the chief object of the state. There consequently prevailed between them and the masses a somewhat fierce animosity. When a revolution took place in a Greek state, it was generally either a rising against an oligarchy of rich men, or else an attempt on the part of rich men to overthrow democratic government: hence the attempts of the lawgiver to enforce equality in living, so as to prevent the rich man from making, in his mode of life, any outward display of his wealth. In Sparta Lycurgus went so far as to make all eat at the same table. But the idea of the sacredness of property, as we hold it, can hardly be said to have existed in the ancient communities. Dispossessions, confiscations, redistributions, were not uncommon. The power of the lender over the borrower's person was from the earliest times, both in Greece and in Rome, very great, and kept alive the discontent of the poor, making it extremely important for the rich man everywhere to get and keep possession of the government. It was only by getting hold of the administration of the law that he could feel absolutely secure.

To understand this more completely, we have to bear in mind that there is no record of a poor aristocracy having long retained possession of any state. In spite of the definition of the word which makes aristocrats the best men in the community, all attempts to maintain an aristocracy very long in power without wealth have proved failures. A poor nobility, even when it has a court and a standing army to support it, is

never well able to justify itself in the popular
eye. The people expect a powerful man to live
with a certain ostentation. He has to have very
commanding talents or to render great services,
in order to live simply, without loss of political
prestige. Consequently, notwithstanding what
long and illustrious descent might do for a man,
the Greek definition of oligarchy or aristocracy
as rich men was not far wrong. There is
something a little ridiculous about the poor nobleman, and he has been in all ages extensively
caricatured, and his pretensions to eminence have
been mocked at.

When, in the beginning of this century, the
result of the French Revolution had discredited
democracy as a cure for modern ills, there naturally and speedily arose among the champions of
aristocracy a desire to discredit ancient democracy also as an example for the modern world,
and modern writers speedily took sides between
the Greek rich and the Greek poor. More particularly, a history of Greece written by Mr.
Mitford, and published in 1810, seemed to have
for its special object to show the failure of Athe-
nian democracy, and to warn the modern advocates of popular government of the danger of
their theories. He was apparently producing
a good deal of effect, and was having his own
way, when George Grote, then a young man,

appeared on the scene with an article criticising
him (in the "Westminster Review" of April,
1826) that excited a sensation which we in later
days find it difficult to understand.   He over-
whelmed the historian with Greek learning, —
with his minute knowledge of all that could be
known concerning Greek manners, ideas, history,
geography, and literature.   The article was not
very long, but it was conclusive, and after its
appearance Mitford ceased to have authority.
But in spite of Thirlwall's more impartial view
and of Grote's own vindication of Greek popular
government in his history, Athens continued to
be, in the eyes of many conservatives, an example of the dangers of a government of the
majority, until a comparatively recent period.
Democracy had certainly to contend with powerful illustrations of the superiority of the government of the few in the matter of continuity of
policy, to be found in the history of states like
Venice, Berne, and Geneva, where public affairs
were administered with apparent success for centuries, by a minority of patricians.   All these
fell, not directly through their own weakness so
much as through the French Revolution, which
may be said to have swept them away by force.
But in any case they could not have survived
the gradual growth of cheap literature.   The
success of aristocratic policy everywhere is due,

in large part, to the possibility of secrecy, and to the possibility of administering through few counselors and without much discussion. The existence and expression of such a thing as " public opinion " — that is, the opinion of a great number of people, most of them ill informed as to the matter in hand, — are fatal to it. The boldness which has always been one of the marks of aristocratic government is, in fact, due largely to the belief that it knows exactly how the few feel, whose feeling about any matter is of importance. If the multitude had to be consulted, this boldness would be impossible, owing to uncertainty as to what the final tribunal would think. Consequently, the rise of the newspaper press — furnishing to every man the materials for an opinion of some sort about public affairs, and the opportunity to say something about them, whether well or ill judged — had naturally a paralyzing effect on aristocratic policy, and would have led to the downfall of aristocratic states even if the French Revolution had never occurred. The contentment with material conditions, such as the careful administration of the finances and of justice, and the general security that were characteristics of a government like that of Berne, would have disappeared rapidly before the popular desire to share in the government. This would have been the inevitable result of popular knowledge of what authority was doing which the cheap press brought with it. When every man in the state knew, or thought he knew, what ought to be done, the period of government by small trained minorities had passed away.

But as I have said, independently of this influence of the printing-press, the eighteenth century closed with the revelation of great aristocratic failures all over Europe. The states which Napoleon overthrew were all administered by a few men of aristocratic birth with but indifferent success. The break-down of their régime in France was made notorious by the terrible way in which popular discontent found expression. But in nearly every country on the Continent, outside Switzerland, privilege reigned supreme, with harsh, even contemptuous treatment of the poor, and with little or no economy in the administration of the finances, except for military purposes. Indeed, in every state on the Continent the government may be said to have failed, even as an instrument for carrying on war with its neighbors. All its political arrangements seem to have been made simply for the purpose of enabling a small class to enjoy themselves, and to indulge in their favorite amusement of commanding armies.

In the discussion which arose out of the great

uprising at the end of the century, therefore, there was little or nothing to be said for the old régime. The most was made of the excesses of the Revolution, but no defense was possible of what the Revolution overturned. It was not surprising, then, that the supporters of the old régime should turn to Athens for examples of what the popular movement was likely to lead to if the world chose to abandon its ancient ways. What this abandonment would mean it is difficult for us to conceive now, in an age when birth has lost its prestige, and the distinction between the *manant* and the nobleman has become almost diverting. The only places in which it survives with any power are Austria and Germany, particularly Austria, in which the noble class, or class with a "sixteen quarterings," still lives apart, and monopolizes many of the offices of state and much of the command of the army, as it did in France before the Revolution.

Nearly everywhere, however, even in as democratic states as ours, aristocracy leaves traditions which are strong enough to make the rich desire to inherit them. All over the modern world the desire to belong to a class apart, with other needs than those of the masses, and with claims to consideration not possessed by the not-rich, the tendency to consider themselves in some way superior to the rest of the community, is one of the marks of the wealthy. And this claim on the part of the rich to be the heirs of the old aristocracy, and to possess the same social though perhaps not the same political value, constitutes one of the dangers of the time. Everywhere the rich man seeks in some way, generally by marriage, to ally himself with the old aristocracy and be absorbed into it, and he demands whatever social deference used to be accorded to birth. Tocqueville makes some gentle fun of the American's disposition to trace his descent from a noble family of the same name in England; and the tendency of well-to-do Americans to ally themselves, immediately on landing in Europe, with the old order of nobility is described by Laboulaye in the pleasantry, " Un Yankee à Paris se croit né gentilhomme."

EQUALITY

THE event which first gave the idea of democracy a recognized place in the modern world was the embodiment of the American Declaration of Independence in political revolution. There has been a great deal of discussion as to the origin of the doctrine of the equality of men which it proclaims, and it is a point of some interest for the political philosopher, as Sir Henry Maine has shown. But its history as a political dogma is not really important, because it must have been in the air all over modern Europe after the spread of Christianity. It was impossible to teach Christianity to any man without leading him to think himself as good as anybody. The great importance which the Christian religion attaches to the future of the soul, and its bold affirmation of the equality of souls after death, must have led even slaves, in the earlier ages, to put themselves secretly on the same plane, before the Creator, with kings and senators and noblemen. Macaulay's florid description of the Puritan's attitude towards " kings and priests " fairly represented, doubtless, the state of mind of thousands, if not of millions,

for centuries. What was wanting was the physical power to procure recognition of the doctrine
from the state, so dominating was the influence
of prescription, tradition, and custom. So that
there is every likelihood that its production by a
community in arms, no matter for what reason,
was simply the expression of a thought which
was already popular in the sense of being widely
held.

That it had at that time the signification
which we are now so apt to attach to it — not
only that all men are born equal, but that for
public purposes one man's opinion is as good as
that of any other man, and that there is as much
reason for consulting him regarding common
affairs as any other man — is not probable. The
state of the world in the eighteenth century warrants the belief that what men meant by equality
at that time was equality of burdens, the abolition of all exemptions from the common liabilities and of all privileges in running the race of
life. This was really the kind of equality of
which both the American and the French Revolution were the expression in the beginning. I
conclude this from the readiness in both, at the
outset, to follow and obey the lead of men of
mark; the recognition of the wider range of
experience which education and property give a
man, or may give him, and his generally greater

fitness to lead in politics, which prevailed at that
time.   This was a characteristic, in particular,
of the American Revolution.   It was conducted
largely with loyal support from the masses, under the direction of men of some social distinction.   The class of " notables " seems to have
held its place in the community, undisturbed by
political events.   The English tradition that a
prominent social station entitles a man to some
sort of political leadership, or at all events to
high office, does not seem to have been really
broken down, or even to have been strongly
assailed, until Andrew Jackson's time, when the
doctrine of equality took on a new form, and
found for the first time full expression in our
politics.

Equality, as every one acknowledges, is the
foundation of democracy.   It means democracy
when it gets itself embodied in law.   When all
are equal, there is no reason why all should not
rule.   But the equality of the French in 1792,
when the revolutionary government was established, was something different from the equality
of 1789.   In 1789 the equality which was asked
for was, in the main, simply an equality of rights
and burdens between the nobility and the *tiers
état*.   Equality, as Montesquieu uses the term,
means simply love, not of one's order, but of
one's country, and as such he made it the equiva-

lent of democracy. <u>Democracy, he says, *is* equality</u>. But the word "equality" for him evidently had no social signification. It meant rather equality of service to the country: that every one was held to the same amount of public duty, according to his means, and that every one was entitled to the same opportunities of taking part in the government. That being born of particular parents made any one essentially of better quality than anybody else; that if one hundred babies of different conditions were brought up in the same manner, the sons of noblemen or gentlemen among them would show their superiority to the others in their character, was a doctrine which, after the Middle Ages, was probably never fully accepted even by the most ardent believers in heredity. Every generation was witness of the break-down, if I may use the expression, of the principle of heredity. That is to say, a large number of noble or gentle families in every generation lost their position or property, because the founder did not transmit his qualities of mind or character to his descendants. The folly or extravagance or imprudence which led to this social *déchéance* was generally due to marked departures in intellect or morals from the original type. The believers in heredity were misled by the analogy of the breeding of animals. Horses transmitted speed and bottom, birds peculiar appearance, with extraordinary certainty. Therefore, it was concluded, a man was likely to have his father's wisdom, or foresight, or mental strength. But his descendants rarely inherit from a father more than one or two mental peculiarities, valuable when united with other things, but, standing alone, of little use in the battle of life, — a fact which may be verified anywhere by observing the families of distinguished men. A man eminent in politics, or law, or medicine, or commerce, or finance, or war, is seldom succeeded by a son who recalls the *ensemble* of qualities which have secured the father's success, although he may have one or two of his characteristics. Heredity obtained its stronghold in the popular imagination in the Middle Ages, owing to the fact that the son was in possession of the father's power when he died, and that in a rude age, when things were mainly decided by fighting, it offered the readiest means of settling peaceably questions of succession. But as soon as the question of the right of a class to rule in virtue of heredity became a subject of discussion, heredity broke down. It was a custom which was valuable in the time of its origin, but, like most customs, found it impossible to justify itself by any better argument than that, under some circumstances, it had produced good results.

But in America, from the settlement of the colonies, the English doctrine that distinction should serve in place of heredity seems to have held its place in the popular imagination. The founding of colonies, the making of conquests, the growth of trade and commerce, and the early practice of admitting able lawyers to the House of Lords had familiarized Englishmen with the idea of a man's making his fortune by some sort of adventure, no matter what his origin. The peers, too, sapped their own power unconsciously by making legislators of young men of promise, no matter of what extraction, and giving them seats in the House of Commons. The result was that the association, in the English mind, of men of mark of some kind with office-holding and the work of government took deep root after the revolution of 1640, and was transferred to America. It was generally leading men of prominence and character who were made governors and judges, and were sent to the legislature and to Washington. The Revolution was carried through, and the Constitution formed and its adoption brought about, by men of this kind. The idea of an obscure man, of a man who was not lifted above the crowd in some way, being fit for the transaction of public affairs was still unfamiliar. All the members of the Constitutional Convention were men of some local note, and so were the earlier administrators of the new government.

This, too, down to that period, had been the strongest tradition of all previous democracies. All democracies, both ancient and modern, had made a practice of electing to office, not always their best men, but their most prominent men. In none of them had a man who was not in some way raised above the mass of his fellow citizens — who had not succeeded in life, in short — much chance of filling a high or an important place. This was eminently true of Greece and Rome and Switzerland. In a small state, where everybody knows everybody well, and where elections and other public affairs are transacted in the market-place, within sound of an orator's voice, this is not difficult. Office-seekers are, in a measure, compelled to be eloquent, or distinguished for something. An obscure man, or a man whose character bears serious blemishes of some kind, will hardly dare to ask the confidence of the citizens in his fitness for great duties. The composition of the Roman Senate, which from the beginning consisted of notables who had in some manner rendered the state marked service, and the selection for which the people for centuries committed to a magistrate, showed better than almost anything else the desire of the ancient democracies to avail themselves of their best talent. What they seem to have insisted on above all things, in the management of the state, was not the right of filling offices with anybody they pleased, but the right of filling them with their most competent men. It may be said that this was not so great a mark of wisdom as appears, because every ancient democracy was in a position of some danger. It was continually exposed to war and subjugation by some stronger neighbor, and the penalty of defeat in those days was tremendous. The vanquished were killed or sold into slavery, and their women were appropriated by the conquerors. So that the cultivation and recognition of ability were conditions of existence. In the case of Rome this necessity was even stronger than elsewhere, for she entered on a career of conquest from the very beginning, and this called for the filling of the Senate, which decided what was to be conquered and selected generals for the work, with the ablest men in the state.

In nothing does modern democracy differ so much from the ancient democracy as in this indifference to distinction, owing in a large degree to the size of the two communities which fully practice it, and to the great preponderance of the less instructed class in the elections. The Greek democracy, and in a less degree that of

Rome, were composed of a selected body the principal occupation of which was politics, and they were brought in almost daily contact with the leading men of the community, and were consulted by them in the forum concerning both war and peace. We can hardly imagine a better education than this, touching the management of affairs and the qualities which it requires. The consequence was that the people were daily engaged in forming judgments as to the capacity of men with whom they were familiar, and the men were daily engaged in giving *viva voce* reasons for their advice, or explaining and defending their conduct, or setting forth their own claims to an office. Our democracies, on the other hand, are composed of vast bodies of men who have but small acquaintance with the machinery of public affairs, or with the capacity of individuals for managing it.

This brings me to what is probably the greatest danger of modern democracy, if, like all previous régimes, it should lose its hold on popular affections and fall into decay. The spread of democracy — that is, the participation of the whole community in the work of government — has been accompanied by a great increase in the complexity of human affairs. The interdependence of nations through the growth of trade, the increase of literature, the incessant conversation with one another kept up by the press, the greatly improved facilities of travel, has grown to a degree undreamt of even a century ago. A debate in a legislative body, the careless speech of a chief magistrate, a slight change in the system of taxation of even one nation, a small discovery by a man of science in any country, in our time produce an almost instantaneous effect over the whole civilized world; and one might say, the whole world, whether civilized or not, for civilization now asserts the dominion of its ideas everywhere. In truth, the extent to which all news, no matter whence it comes, affects or may affect the lives of most of us is present to every man when he opens his newspaper in the morning. And all private business partakes of this public complexity. The size of all undertakings, either of production or exchange or transportation, is tasking the human faculty of administration to the uttermost, and leads a great many people to suppose that individuals are no longer equal to the task, and that it must be hereafter assumed by the state. For success in any business now, an amount of knowledge is necessary which in the last century hardly one man in a million possessed; decisions must now be made on the moment, for which, a hundred years ago, a merchant might take half a year.

The result is that the government of such a

world need an increase in intellectual equipment corresponding to the increase in business.
The amount of property, too, which is placed at
the disposal of the modern legislator is something beyond calculation. Since the exclusion
of the old landed class from the work of government, a process which began soon after the
French Revolution, the growth of personal property, which to be enjoyed or increased has in
some way to be displayed, and thus comes within
the reach of the government, is one of the most
remarkable phenomena of the modern world.
When the old ruler had taxed land, his resources
were well-nigh exhausted. To-day the number
of movables out of each of which the public
treasury can extract tens of millions, in every
civilized country, has made taxation one of the
nicest of arts. In fact, one has but to read
such a book as Mr. Wells's "Recent Economic
Changes" to see that within a century we have
entered a new material world, a description of
which would have been deemed fantastic even
in 1800. In every field of human activity we
have drawn heavily on the supply of administrative talent. Whether it wishes to command
a great army or a great fleet, or to conduct a
great business, every state has to search its entire
population to get a man fit for the work. In
some things in which capacity is not easy to

test, such as war, most countries remain, pending the outbreak of hostilities, in anxious uncertainty as to the capacity of their military men, by sea or by land.

We must remember, too, that this great increase of affairs, this vast growth of trade and commerce, is made possible by the creation of what is called " credit." Without credit, in spite of the improvements in transportation and in the transmission of intelligence, we could not have had this expansion of business. All the gold and silver in the world would not have been sufficient. We have had to call into use men's faith in the fulfillment of one another's pledges, so that modern prosperity has come to rest, in the main, on written promises or letters of private individuals, saying they will pay a certain amount of money, or deliver a certain quantity of goods, on a day named. The result is a great structure of what may be called mutual faith, of extraordinary delicacy, which the slightest suspicion that the world will not continue to go on in the way in which it is going on, that there will be a war or an earthquake or a startling piece of legislation, may overthrow at any moment. In fact, it would perhaps be more accurate to compare it to a network covering the whole earth, than to a building. The slightest derangement or break in it anywhere is

felt everywhere else, and may involve great de-
preciation of property, and the postponement or
abandonment of enterprises of great importance.
The care of it, the avoidance of all measures or
movements likely to disturb it, has, therefore,
in our day, to be one of the first cares of a
statesman.   To be fully aware, however, of the
importance of credit, either actual experience of
the work of exchange or theoretical knowledge
of it from study is necessary.   An ignorant man
or a small farmer, who knows nothing of any
dealings but cash dealings, finds it difficult to
understand its importance, and may be frequently tempted to take steps in administration
and legislation seriously detrimental to it, without meaning or foreseeing any harm.

As I have already said, the really alarming
feature connected with the growth of democracy
is, that it does not seem to make adequate provision for the government of this new world.
Its chief function, like the chief function of the
monarch whom it has succeeded, is to fill offices.
This is the chief function of the sovereign
power everywhere, no matter by what name it is
called.   To find the right men for the public
places is almost the only work which falls, or has
ever fallen, to the ruler.   It is by the manner in
which this is done, more than by the laws which
are passed, that the goodness or badness of a

government is tested. If the functionaries are honest and faithful, almost any kind of political constitution is endurable. If they are ignorant or tyrannical or corrupt, the best constitution is worthless. If we listen to the conversation of any group of men who are condemning a political system, we shall find that their talk consists mainly of reports of malfeasance in office, of officials having done things which they ought not to have done, and of their having failed to do things which they ought to have done. Government is an impalpable abstraction except as it makes itself felt through functionaries, which is about the same thing as saying that administration is even more important than legislation, that even bad laws well executed hardly work as much unhappiness as good laws badly executed.

The first effect of this great change on democracy was delight at finding that government places and commissions in the army were no longer the monopoly of the aristocracy, that family or wealth was no longer a necessary qualification for them, and that the influences through which they might be procured were within the reach of the poor or lowly born. The tide of democratic opinion has ever since been in favor of the increase of offices. In France, in Italy, and in the United States, every government has found that this increase was a popular

measure, and has given way to the temptation
of strengthening itself by the bestowal of them.
The passion for them, even where the tenure is
brief or insecure, has apparently grown with
their number. The tradition of the old régime,
that a man who represented the government was
in some way superior to the people with whom
he came in contact, has apparently, in the popular eye, clung to the places. Then, the certainty of the salary to the great multitude who
in every country either fail in life, or shrink
from the conflicts which the competitive system
makes necessary, is very attractive; it soon con-
verted the civil service into what has been called
" spoils ; " that is, booty won by victories at the
polls.

It is easy to see that the only way to meet this
necessary growth of demand for offices was to
adhere to the old system of applying to the management of state affairs the principle which
reigns in business, that of securing the best talent available ; and of giving the chief places,
at least, to men who had already made a mark in
the world by success in some field of activity.
This, as I have said, was the rule of the democracies of the ancient world. To preserve for
the democratic government the old respect and
authority which used to surround the monarchical government, it was absolutely necessary to

compete vigorously, through both money and honors, in the labor market, with private business, the demands of which on the community's store of talent became very great as soon as steam and electricity were brought into the service of commerce and manufactures. But the tendency has not run in this direction. As regards the lower offices, the duties of which are easily comprehensible by everybody, and are merely matters of routine, in which discretion or judgment plays little part, there has been in this country a decided return to the tests of ordinary business, such as character and competency, and a decided revival of confidence in such motives as security of tenure and the prospect of promotion. But as regards the higher or elective offices, such as those of legislators and governors, the tendency to discredit such qualifications as education and special experience has been marked. In the popular mind there is what may be called a disposition to believe not only that one man is as good as another, but that he knows as much on any matter of general interest. In any particular business the superiority of the man who has long followed it is freely acknowledged, but in public affairs this is not perhaps so much denied as disregarded. One of the oddest characteristics of the silver movement was the general refusal to accept the experience of any country or age as instructive, and this in a matter in which all light comes from experience. Bryan's proclamation that the opinion of all the professors in the United States would not affect his opinions in the least was an illustration of this great self-confidence of a large democracy. In a small democracy this could hardly have occurred.

All the great modern democracies have to contend almost for existence against the popular disposition to treat elective offices as representative, and to consider it of more importance that they should be filled by persons holding certain opinions or shades of opinion than by persons most competent to perform their duties. The distinction between representing and administering seems plain enough; and yet, since the French Revolution, the democratic tendency has been everywhere to obscure it. This has not unnaturally led to the idea that the offices are rewards for the persons who have done most to propagate or defend certain views, and ought to be given to them independently of their fitness. To this confusion of two different functions I must ascribe the deterioration which has been remarked so frequently in the legislatures of all democratic countries in modern times. The number of men of experience or special knowledge, as well as of conspicuous men, which they contain, seems to decline steadily, and the number of interests committed to their charge as steadily to increase.

The disregard of special fitness, combined with unwillingness to acknowledge that there can be anything special about any man, which is born of equality, constitutes the great defect of modern democracy. That large communities can be successfully administered by inferior men is a doctrine which runs directly counter not only to the experience of the race, but to the order appointed for the advance of civilization, which has been carried forward almost exclusively by the labor of the fittest, despite the resistance or reluctance of the unfit. This order of nature, too, has been recognized fully in private affairs of every description. In all of them competency on the part of administrators is the first thing sought for, and the only thing trusted. But in private affairs the penalty of any disregard of this rule comes quickly; in public affairs the operation of all causes is much slower, and their action is obscure. Nations take centuries to fall, and the catastrophe is preceded by a long period of the process called " bad government," in which there is much suffering and alarm, but not enough to make the remedy plain. France furnishes the best modern illustration of this rule. The causes of the

Revolution undoubtedly began to operate at the majority of Louis XIV., but for over one hundred years their nature and certain results were not perceived, in spite of the great popular suffering which prevailed during the whole period.

The worst of the slowness of this decadence is that it affects national character to a degree which makes recovery more difficult, even after the origin and nature of the disease have become plain. Men soon get accustomed to the evils of their condition, particularly if there is nobody in particular to blame. The inaction or negligence or shortcomings of great numbers assume the appearance of a law of nature, or of repeated failures or attempts at the impossible. The apparent difficulty of reform, except by catastrophe or revolution, begets either despondency or over-cheerfulness.

THE NOMINATING SYSTEM

IT would hardly be possible to write a better description of the actual machinery of our nominating system than Mr. James Bryce's in his "American Commonwealth." In what I am about to say of it, therefore, I shall take for granted that the reader is familiar with it, or has abundant means of making himself acquainted with its working. Every American has either practical or theoretical knowledge of the process by which we select men for office. There are probably few Americans who have not either participated in it, or been exhorted to do so by writers on political morality. In fact, presence at the primary meetings, under the general name of " attending to his political duties," has been much preached as the chief political duty of the busy man who does not otherwise take an active part in politics. It used to be held more strongly than it is now that if a man had taken part in a primary, he might always, with a good conscience, vote for the candidate whom the primary and its resulting conventions presented to him. The primary has gradually assumed in our system the air of a scheme or device on which the

republic rests. Of course it has differed in its
character and composition in different parts of
the country; but under whatever name, for at
least half a century, it has been treated by most
political philosophers, as well as by practical politicians, as the fundamental fact of our politics,
indifference to which on the part of the intelligent is the cause of nearly all our woes. For
some years, in many of the discussions which
abuses have excited, writers have been apt to
ascribe, especially in the cities, the particular
trouble under consideration to the refusal of
respectable citizens to take part in the primaries.
This refusal has even been more dwelt on than
the abstention at elections, which this class have
practiced on a large scale. Yet the primary
meeting, as the source of the nominating convention, is a novelty in democracy. It is, strictly
speaking, simply part of a new system of selecting candidates for office, as such is evidently an
experiment, and is not necessarily a part of the
democratic scheme of government. It is of the
essence of the democratic system that the majority shall decide who shall hold and administer
the various administrative and legislative offices,
but the mode of choosing candidates for these
offices is a matter which democracy leaves completely open. Nomination is the offer to the
people of the services of certain persons. But

the democratic principle does not define the manner in which these persons shall be picked out.

Accordingly, almost every kind of nomination for office has prevailed in democratic countries. The earliest and most natural is the one which has for the most part been in use in small democracies, — the selection for places of dignity or responsibility of persons eminent in the eyes of their fellow-citizens for what is called "social station;" that is, generally acknowledged superiority of some kind, in private life. This is the plan to which nearly all communities resort in their more primitive and simpler stage. They single out men who have in some satisfactory manner raised themselves above their fellows, and have become what is called "distinguished." These are supposed to have a kind of moral right to offices which impose responsibility. In this stage, and in this stage only, is it true that the office, as the saying is, seeks the man, not the man the office. The agreement of his fellow-citizens that he is the person whom the place or the work demands is a kind of recognition which the great man waits for, as most agreeable to him. This system prevailed in the beginning in all the small democracies of Greece and of Switzerland. And we have a suggestion as to the manner of nominations in New England in the early days, in the account by Gordon, the historian, of the life of Samuel Adams, the New England agitator, where he says that in 1724 Adams's father "and about twenty others, one or two from the north end of the town, where all ship business was carried on, used to meet, make a caucus, and lay their plans for introducing certain persons to places of trust and power."

In the next stage the candidate does not wait for this recognition; he offers himself for the place or honor. Both recognition and honor are desired, and he therefore nominates himself; that is, he calls public attention to his own fitness, and sets forth with what fidelity and efficiency he would perform the duties which the office might devolve on him. In a small democracy, this, as a rule, is all that is necessary. Having heard what the rival candidates, if there are rivals, have to say for themselves, the voters make their choice. The election comes quickly, if not immediately, after the nomination. People are supposed to be able to form a prompt judgment on the matter in hand. There may be intrigues in the candidate's behalf, but what we call the "canvass," or long process of persuasion, is not necessary and does not exist.

As the number of voters grows larger, the candidate is not left wholly to his own merits, or exertions, or reputation. A committee is ap-

pointed to look after his interests, and a canvass
begins, for which the committee make arrangements. The members go themselves among the
electors, or employ others to do so, to make sure,
first, that the electors will vote for somebody,
and then that this somebody shall be their own
man. The nature of the arguments employed
in his favor has probably never varied since the
practice of electing candidates began. They are
the arguments by which the voter is most likely
to be influenced, no matter of what kind. It
was through the canvass that the great and
powerful first learned to conciliate the poor and
lowly, and from the earliest times the various
modes employed to cajole them have been a
favorite subject of satirists. The first large democracy with which we have any acquaintance
was that of England in the eighteenth century.
Elections had been held before that time, and
the democratic spirit had prevailed in them, but
it was only in the eighteenth century that they
became really an important instrument of government, and the wealthy began to think it
worth their while to use their money to influence
the result. The contests were generally between
landed proprietors and their connections, and
the intrusion of a man like Burke into politics,
on the ground of mere eloquence or ability, was
a rare incident. Very soon elections began to

determine the fate of ministries and influence the complexion of the House of Commons. Persuasion by argument was largely abandoned for bribery, and the use of the mob of non-electors for purposes of violence and intimidation became common. It was only in great cities, like London and Bristol, that men like Burke and Wilkes were able to displace the men of property or high connections, and we have in Burke's address to the electors of Bristol probably the first specimen of a real argumentation from a candidate to the voters of a large constituency, without appeals to some sort of prejudice.

In America, the old method of the candidacy of local magnates, selected for the purpose by other men like themselves, their neighbors and friends, seems to have prevailed long after the settlement of the country. The practice of the English counties was preserved; that is, the selection by some people of influence — sometimes, in New England, the clergy — of a good person to send to the legislature or to fill any other elective office. In all the colonies, and for some years in all the states, offices were reserved naturally for men of local mark, generally created by property and social position. In all small communities, it is property which gives most distinction. In fact, from the fall of the Roman Empire almost to our time, the world was governed by property, and property was mainly land, and was associated in the popular mind, to a degree which we now find it difficult to understand, with political power and prominence. A landless man was held to have no " stake in the country," and therefore to have no right to manage public affairs. " Broad acres" became a synonym for wealth, and a natural title to political authority and confidence. This idea prevailed in the settlement of America, and found expression in large grants of land in several of the colonies. Probably nothing did as much to democratize America as the abundance of land and the ease of its acquisition. People began to perceive that a large landowner was not necessarily a great man, and the idea of government by landholders, which had held possession of the world for a thousand years, was killed by the perception. Of course this dispossession of the landholder was aided by the growth of personal property, through the progress of trade, commerce, and invention. The freeholder has never stood as high in politics as he did during the seventeenth and eighteenth centuries. Thereafter, realty had to contend with personalty for influence in government.

America thus came out of the Revolution with the old and, one may say, human plan of treating some kind of previous social distinction, already known to the voters, as giving a title to nomination for office. The neighbors met and talked over the proper persons to fill certain places, and the ministers and persons in office gave advice. This is, as I have said, the human plan, which has always had recognition in business. Commercial agents and persons charged with trusts were always chosen in this way. Personal knowledge of the man by those holding the power of appointment was considered necessary. It seemed difficult, in small communities, to think of any other way. That a man was fit for office who was not already raised above his fellows, either by character or by the possession of property, was an unfamiliar idea. Nearly all the Revolutionary leaders were men of this kind. The signers of the Declaration of Independence and the drafters of the Constitution were all local notables. They were marked out for their work by some sort of prominence in their own homes. For nearly fifty years after the new government had been set up, nominees were known to everybody. Even nominees for the presidency were suggested by Congress, as state officers were in like manner suggested by the legislatures, the members of which were generally the men most prominent in their own localities. Why legislators had this weight and were allowed to assume this function may be

conjectured from the size of the vote.   In 1792
the vote for the governor of New York was
only about 16,000, but by 1824 it had risen to
83,000.   The growth of population diminished
the number of well-known men, and the congressional caucus, which was simply a private meeting for the purpose of talking over common
affairs, took on itself, not unnaturally, the duty
of suggesting to the constituencies the names
of candidates for the presidency.   This practice
appears to have begun as early as 1796, and by
1800 it had become so overbearing that the
presidential electors provided for by the Constitution, virtually ceased to have power or authority.

But the constituencies rapidly grew restless
under congressional dictation.   In 1808, a summons issued by Senator Bradley, of Vermont,
"in pursuance of the power vested in him as
president of the late convention of the Republican members of both Houses of Congress," was
violently resented by Mr. Gray, a Virginia member, who "took the earliest opportunity to de-
clare his abhorrence of the usurpation of power
declared to be vested in him (Bradley), of his
mandatory style and the object contemplated,"
and claimed for "the people" the right of
"selecting persons to fill the important offices."
In 1800, when a few members met and pledged

themselves to use their influence in support of Jefferson, they were denounced as a "Jacobinical conclave,"[1] an expression for which the publisher was brought to the bar of the Senate. The congressional caucus, however, continued for twenty years to do the work of nomination, though with increasing hesitation and timidity, and amidst growing discontent with its action. The Clintonian platform in New York in 1812 declared " its opposition to nomination of chief magistrates by congressional caucus, as well because such practices are the exercise of undelegated authority, as of their repugnance to the freedom of elections." The caucus tried to defend itself by proclaiming that its members met only in their individual capacity, and that its nominations were simply suggestions. The attendance on it, also, by individual members of the party, was fitful. Meetings seldom contained more than two thirds of those who might have been present.

The first suggestion of a nominating convention seems to have come from the " New York American," which in 1822 proposed a general convention of Republican delegates to assemble in Washington a few months before election day, and nominate a candidate for the presidency. "Coming immediately from their constituents,"

[1] *Niles's Register*, December, 1823.

it said, " they would bring with them the sense
of the people, and they would express that sense
without being influenced by motives that might
sway the representatives in Congress, who during the sessions at the seat of government may
be supposed, without derogation to their purity,
to have formed personal attachments and party
combinations which would render them less fit
for the important duty." It will thus be seen
that the convention was expected to be a body
which, like the constitutional conventions and
the Hartford convention, would meet to discuss,
without foregone conclusions or pledges. After
this, nomination by the congressional caucuses
passed out of use. As late as 1823–24 the
friends of Mr. Crawford, of Georgia, tried to
call a congressional caucus for his nomination ;
but very few members attended, and the project
failed. Nomination by the state legislatures
then began, as a recommendation or mark of
local commendation, in cases where there was
not a general agreement on a particular man,
owing to his eminence in the party. The use
of the nominating convention is ascribed by
Alexander Johnston to the fact that " the new
politicians, whom the rising democratic spirit
and the extension of the suffrage were together
bringing to the front, were determined to try
the issue with the old party leaders in a new

form." [1]   In short, the voters wished to have a share in the work of choosing the candidates whom they were to elect. Social knowledge of these had ceased. It was no longer possible to presume on it. The United States had entered on a new era in its politics.

The establishment and growth of the nominating convention, in truth, constitute the capital fact of modern democracy in America. Of no other political phenomenon has the influence on the government and on the character of public men been so powerful. It is effecting a change in our political manners of which there is no parallel. But there is nothing in American history, of the progress and consequences of which there appears to have been so little prescience. There is no mention or allusion, either in Tocqueville or in any of our early writers, to its probable or possible effect. One finds no allusion to it in any of the commentators on the Constitution, early or late. The fact seems to be that its tendencies were hidden from the country during the reign of men of influence in our politics, such as Clay and Webster and Calhoun, by their own overwhelming importance, and subsequently by the absorbing political interest developed among all classes by the anti-

[1] *Cyclopædia of Political Science:* article, "Nominating Conventions."

slavery contest.   This interest, it may be said, forced foregone conclusions on the conventions. Their work was done before they met, by public sentiment.   They simply registered decrees already issued.   It is since the war that the real working of the convention has been made manifest, and the vastness and complication of the machinery necessary for its production have become fully understood.

It was made necessary in the beginning, as I have said, by the size of the population.   We were making the first attempt in the history of the world to govern a very large population by universal suffrage, and the previous modes of nominating candidates for office either by personal knowledge or by the recommendation of notables, had broken down.   The people had grown too numerous to have personal knowledge of candidates, and they were too democratic to accept the recommendation of any one claiming superior powers of discrimination.   A system of nomination in which every one could take some part seemed to have been made necessary by the circumstances of the country, and the elected convention seemed the fairest and easiest.   Indeed, it was hard then, as it is now, to conceive of any other.

Another fact speedily appeared, and that was that universal suffrage was made more difficult,

as a political agency, through the mere growth
of society. When it was first established, the
electors were a small body who were animated
by great eagerness to vote. In nearly all discussions about the suffrage, in the early part of the
century, it was taken for granted that a great
number of electors would feel the same eagerness to exercise it, as a few. The strong desire
of the excluded masses to make their will known
in this way was the fundamental assumption of
what was called radical politics. It does not
appear to have entered any one's head that there
would ever be difficulty in getting the bulk of
the electors to come to the polls. There were
many fears about the bad influence of their vote
on the government, but there were no fears that
they would not immediately and fully exercise
the privilege conferred on them. In like manner, the canvass, as we call it, or the work of
persuading them to vote in a particular way, did
not seem likely to be arduous. Their number
not being great, it was supposed they could be
easily reached by influential speakers whose
opinions had weight. There was no trouble, for
instance, in getting at the 16,000 of the State
of New York in 1792, except the trouble of
traveling, which really gave electioneering a
gravity in those days of which we now know
nothing. A man who comes by an express train

to talk to us cannot seem as serious an apostle as the man who comes by stage, or on horseback. His place, in our day, is only inadequately filled by the swarm of young orators whom each party lets loose at the opening of a political campaign, who are rarely known to the body of the electors, and are listened to with the lukewarm attention which is all that a man who has not already made his mark can claim.

As the number of electors increased, too, the mere machinery of elections became more complicated. The early practice of *viva voce* voting, which was simple and natural in the days when each man either was entitled to vote as he pleased, or owed his vote to somebody else, threw a large part of the trouble on the voter. But the ballot, which was well known in the ancient world, and was adopted by most of the American colonies, as numbers grew, threw greatly enlarged responsibility on governments. The provision of ballots and their distribution, and the enactment of precautions against fraud, which is much easier with ballots than in *viva voce* voting, made elections more complicated than they were in earlier days.

All this helped to increase the importance of the nominating convention. The work of finding candidates to please this growing multitude, and of making it seem worth their while to par-

ticipate in the contest, became more and more
heavy.   One result of this work was to raise the
value of party in the popular estimation.   It
was soon discovered that party spirit was a great
assistance in managing large bodies of voters.
For one thing, it greatly diminished the active
work of canvassing.   It was found, as voters
increased in number, that the work of persuading or influencing was much lightened by party
fidelity.   To have a party, and be accustomed
to act with it, helps the great body of voters in
modern times in making up their minds what to
do at elections, and in fact what to do in any
matter of common concern with others.   It is only
the few who have firm opinions about anything
but their own affairs.   About public affairs
the majority need the strengthening influence
of agreement with others, — a fact of human
nature in which, probably, party takes its rise.
There is a certain feeling of pride and of strength
and importance in belonging to an organized
body of any sort, whether a regiment, a club, or
a union, as we see in the multitude of associations which spring up in a free country, and
which the mass of men love to join.   As soon
as you have secured a man's devotion to his
party, either through respect for its principles,
or through pride in its action on some great
occasion, or through admiration of its leaders, or

through liking for that portion of it with which he comes in contact, the task of getting him to support its platform or candidates is greatly lightened. Indeed, argument ceases to be necessary. A presumption that the party is always right, even when it seems to him at the first blush wrong, arises in his mind. He becomes what is known as "a lifelong Democrat" or "a lifelong Republican;" that is, a Democrat or a Republican who does not need to be convinced at every election, but who, having been satisfied early in life that his party was the best party, remains convinced, no matter how the platform may at first run counter to his beliefs, or how much he may disapprove of the candidates. In this way, large numbers of persons who have not time or head for politics, remain always confirmed and unshakable conservatives or radicals.

This is interesting as throwing some light on the nature and origin of what is called "loyalty," — a feeling of attachment to a ruler in virtue of his office that was unknown to the ancient world, but has played a prominent part in the politics of the mediæval and modern world. Loyalty does not really depend upon the character of a ruler, but upon his filling a certain office through hereditary title. The prince still remains entitled to as much devotion as the follower is capable of, no matter what the royal conduct may be. To meet the chance of his behaving badly, the fiction of bad advisers was invented, and grew into the ministerial responsibility of limited monarchies. The king can do no wrong except through the suggestions of bad men, whose removal from his councils restores the power of his natural inclination to do right. The transfer of this feeling of loyalty to party has been accomplished within the present century in the American democracy. There is no doubt that in the early days of the government what is called "party spirit" ran high, but it consisted mainly in abhorrence or detestation of the principles of the other party, rather than in devotion to or admiration of one's own. That the party had not become the power it now is, we see from the ease and swiftness with which both the Federalist and Whig parties disappeared under the influence of mistakes or adversity. The history of both Whigs and Democrats at a later period, however, shows that the feeling of party devotion was rapidly growing. Down to the outbreak of the war, the number of those who were hereditary Whigs or hereditary Democrats — that is, Whigs or Democrats because their fathers were, just like the old Jacobites in England or the Legitimists in France — was large. Men told you how they were brought up to admire Jackson or admire Clay, and were therefore under a sort of romantic obligation to vote the Democratic ticket or the Whig ticket, and to approve of measures fathered by either of the parties.

After the war, the Republican party, which had really taken the place of the Whig party, came out of the conflict with claims on popular confidence and gratitude for which there is no parallel in political history except those of the English Whigs after the Revolution of 1688. It had saved from an immense disaster a great number of things which the nation valued, and there followed from this a strong presumption of its wisdom and virtue. It consequently retains the devotion of a large body of the nation in spite of errors or mishaps; but so does the Democratic party; men vote both tickets in large bodies, without reference to measures or men, under the influence of simple party loyalty. Even in the government of cities, when affairs in no way connected with national politics are under discussion, it is found very difficult to get them considered from any but the federal party point of view. Men vote as Democrats or as Republicans about the police or the gas or the mayor, and can give no reason except that this is what they have always done.

Now, this party loyalty, this confidence that one's own party is the best party to have power, is the basis of the present mode of management, and the origin of what is called " the machine." It is the confidence of the managers that they may rely on loyalty to the party to secure votes, however weak may be their title, which makes the machine possible. The machine consists of one or a dozen men in each county or district, charged with the duty of seeing that party loyalty is kept alive under all circumstances, of seeing that all persons entitled to vote do vote in a certain way, and of protecting them against the influence of hostile arguments, or it may be of giving them a taste of these advantages of loyalty at once, by promises of employment, or of advertising, or of cash, or of custom, or of patronage. The machine, therefore, is constantly working against and discrediting discussion, either of men or of measures. Loyalty does not discuss; it acts, and it has a certain contempt for the balancing of arguments. Given party loyalty and the nominating convention, and the creation of the machine becomes easy.

But in creating the machine a beginning is made with the primary. The hypothesis that one's own party is always the best party rests on another hypothesis: that in every district the primary is attended by all those who have a right to attend it, and that they take part in its proceedings. The falsehood of this assumption is notorious. A fair sample of what may or does happen in the cities was afforded by an examination made by twenty-five leading Republicans into the conduct of the Republican primaries in New York in 1895. It was thereby shown that frauds in the proceedings were practiced on a very great scale ; that large numbers of persons voted at the primaries who had no right to do so ; and that an enrollment secured in this way was, the investigators said, unworthy of "serious attention." That this happens continuously in the great cities there is no reason to doubt. But exposures of this kind are made only occasionally, because exposures come from internal dissensions, the quarrels of two factions within the party. These differences rarely arise about measures. They are generally caused by disputes about offices. As long as there is no disagreement on this point, little is revealed about the constitution or procedure of the primaries in the cities. In the case here cited, although the frauds were brought to light after an elaborate investigation, nothing was ever done to punish them or prevent their having effect. The delegates thus elected took part in the presidential nomination almost without remonstrance.

But the attendance of persons who have no right to vote at primaries is not more remarkable or frequent than the non-attendance of those who have the right. In the cities the proportion of the actual vote cast to the total enrollment is rarely over one third. In the country the same thing happens. From inquiries I have made of competent authorities, it would appear that even in New England the attendance of the voters at the party primaries is very small.

I mention New England because it is the part of the country in which American political customs have arisen, and in which the most serious view has always been taken of politics. New York and Pennsylvania may be said to represent more distinctly than any other part of the country what America is to be hereafter in the matter of wealth and population, and complexity of interests, and the growth of great cities. The cities are everywhere gaining on the country in number of inhabitants; that is, the population is becoming more and more urban, and we may therefore conclude that the smaller towns, as they grow, will become more and more assimilated in political manners and customs to New York, Philadelphia, and Chicago, and will exercise a controlling influence on the government. To check this prospective preponderance, the recently amended Constitution of New York contains a provision that what is to be the Greater New York shall never contribute more than half the members of the Senate. So that the difficulty of securing the attendance of voters at the primaries, in so far as it is affected by numbers, is likely to increase rather than diminish, and the importance of party loyalty to the managers of parties is likely to grow, providing the present system of nomination continues.

This failure on the part of the bulk of the voters to attend the primaries for the purpose of participating in the choice of candidates appears to be due to causes not foreseen by the earlier Democrats. One is the decreased interest in politics caused by increased individual activity and complexity of private affairs. The contrast between the world at the beginning of this century and the world in our day consists not less in increase of population than in increase in the number of occupations, in facilities for making money, and in ease of moving from place to place. It is simply impossible, considering the limits of human powers, for a man living in 1897 to feel the same interest in the working of the machinery of his political party as the man living in 1817. The demands of other things on his attention are infinitely greater ; so are his opportunities of improving his condition ; so is the area over which he may extend his activity. The whole world, one may say, is his field. Literature, science, art, invention, philanthropy, make drafts on his attention of which his great-grandfather never dreamed. A good illustration of this change in the world's outlook may be found in Pepys's "Diary." When Pepys, living in the latter part of the seventeenth century, met friends, they were apt to adjourn to a tavern and sing songs together or to one another. This meant scarcity of topics of conversation. Their world was a very small one, in which few things occurred worth talking about. At that time attendance on political primaries would have been a distraction as well as a duty, and the merits of candidates would have been discussed with keen zest. In our day, song-singing to one another, among men, would be looked upon as an extremely silly and uninteresting practice. To the agricultural communities which composed the civilized world at the beginning of this century it would not have seemed so. In brief, private affairs have assumed, in these later days, an importance as compared to public affairs which our forefathers never could have anticipated. This state of things is causing everywhere a demand for government without trouble, or with very little trouble. The demand for good and enlightened government is as great as ever; but the desire for simple government, which can be carried on without drawing largely on the time and attention of the private citizen, is greater than ever. Government was never so much considered as a means to an end, and not as an end in itself, as it is to-day, — a mode of looking at it which goes far to explain the success of " the man on horseback," or dictator, in troubled communities.

From the time of the Reformation until about 1830, men were mainly occupied upon political freedom; the great concern of our day is domestic comfort, what is called success in life, or, in other words, pecuniary independence. We are mainly interested in this. We are eager that all should enjoy it, even the poor. Our questions are social questions. Political liberty has passed into the category of natural and usual things, like railroad traveling. We are now troubled about lodgings, diet, reading-rooms, old age, pensions, and the " living wage." Consequently, there has for a long while been a decreasing interest in politics, except on great occasions, on the part of the busy, active, intelligent portion of the community. This tendency has been strengthened in our country by the slow or imperfect action of the vote on the conduct of public affairs. It is not exciting to vote in November for a congressman who will have no influence on legislation or administration for a year to come. This is the arrangement of an older world, and one very different from ours.

This is also true of the election of legislators or executive officers. One election is as much as the bulk of citizens in the great centres of industry and population are willing to give time to. The number of abstentions from the polls among the intelligent classes in cities is very great. But the mere selection of candidates under our present system involves two elections, a double demand on time and attention. Experience has shown that the average citizen will not answer this demand. The effect of his vote on a result which is not final is too uncertain to interest him. He dismisses from his mind the whole process of selection, and falls back upon loyalty to his party as a sufficient guide in ordinary times. It is only at periods of great excitement, or great party excess, such as 1860 or 1884, that he troubles himself about, or rises in revolt against, the choice of candidates.

The result of this is that the work of choosing party candidates through the nominating machinery has fallen, as it were naturally, into the hands of an idle class, which either loves political intrigue or does not look further in politics than salaried offices, and a large portion of which consists of men who either have failed in life, or have never had any regular occupation. In their hands the work of nomination has been reduced to a sort of game, of consid-

erable complication, beginning with the holding
of primaries, fraudulent or very thinly attended,
and conducted solely with the view of turning
out a result secretly determined beforehand,
either by a small knot of persons termed " the
machine," or by a single person known as " the
boss," who directs the whole operation.   The
object of the primaries is no longer to express
the will of the party, but to secure for certain
designated persons the support of party loyalty.
The process is based on the confidence of those
who conduct it that, whatever the result may be,
the voters will accept it, for the sake of the
party.   The consequence is that the objections
made originally to nomination by Congress or by
the legislatures — that the nominators are self-
constituted, and that the bulk of the party is
not consulted — are fully applicable to the present mode of nomination.   We have come back,
under much more unfavorable conditions, to the
earlier system, with more than all its faults.

It is a dangerous thing to attempt to describe
causes in politics; that is, to say exactly to what
particular cause any political phenomenon is due.
In truth, it may be said that nothing in politics
has only one cause.   Everything is due to a composition or combination of causes.   The utmost
we can aver is that, of the several agencies which
bring a thing about, one has been unusually

powerful. What we call the machine, for instance, has undoubtedly affected public life and political manners unfavorably; but then the machine could hardly have grown to its present proportions without public apathy; and public apathy, in turn, is due partly to the machine, and partly to the size of the masses which have to be handled and must be persuaded, before any direct effect can be produced. So we find ourselves almost in a vicious circle in accounting for any of the leading features of our democracy. Government is, undoubtedly, the product of the national character; but, on the other hand, it does much to mould the national character. The machine has assumed functions which have to be discharged by somebody, but in discharging them it produces indifference or dislike of the work among the rest of the community. The machine does not persuade. It acts, it arranges, it provides candidates and platforms, but it rather discourages persuasion. It does not support its candidates by arguments, but by appeals to party loyalty. The voter is asked to support this or that candidate, not on account of his principles or character, but because he is the party candidate. But there is nothing in a democracy so important as persuasion. That this work should be well done, and done continuously, is one of the conditions of healthy national life. Indeed, it may be called the heart of democracy, which sends the blood through all the national arteries. As soon as it ceases, circulation becomes languid or intermittent, the political institutions of a country become anæmic, and a dictator, or single ruler of some sort, appears in the distance.

The machine undertakes the work of providing the voter with candidates and getting him to come to the polls, but it does not undertake the previous process of keeping him informed about the rights and wrongs of public questions. It undertakes, if I may say so, to keep party spirit, but not public spirit, alive. It does not attempt any regular work of public instruction. In fact, it discourages discussion, and presents for leadership men clever in management rather than men clever in oratory, men skillful in a certain kind of intrigue for the party benefit, rather than men skillful in propagating ideas of any kind. To this change in the type of the public men I venture to ascribe the frequency of what are called "crazes," of late years; that is, the sudden seizure of the popular mind by enthusiasm for some extravagant idea, or some scheme opposed to human experience and unwarranted by human knowledge. This disappears after a while before what is called "a campaign of education." A campaign of education, such as we have had

to carry on against the greenback movement of
1875, or the excessive tariff of 1890, or the silver craze of 1896, is in reality an attempt to do
in a few months, under stress of some pressing
danger, the work of instruction which should be
constantly going on. This constant persuasion
or instruction must be a condition of all safe
and successful democracy, and to be carried on
fruitfully should be carried on by public men.
In the English democracy, one of the most
wholesome signs of the times, is the incessant
appearance, both before and during the meeting
of Parliament, of public men on the stump. In
fact, addressing his constituents on all the leading questions of the day, home and foreign, is
as much a part of an English leading politician's
functions as sitting in his place in the legislature during the session. It is part, and a most
important part, of popular education. The dis-
continuance of this practice among us is one of
the bad signs of our times. There are but few
of our public men who ever address an audience
except during some exciting canvass, and they
then deal mainly in generalities, such as praise
of their own party or denunciations of the other.
Thorough discussion of distinct measures or
events from all points of view, such as the discussions of the currency question which took
place during the campaign of education in 1896,
is very rare, almost unknown.

It may be said that this work is done by our press, but nothing could be further from the truth. There are but few newspapers which are conducted by men equipped for such work, and there are but few editors, however well equipped, who undertake it; nor does the public expect it of them. The ephemeral and superficial character of the newspaper is so deeply impressed on the popular American mind, that the editor who attempts anything of the kind may almost be said to face a hostile or an indifferent audience. Even if the newspapers do it, they cannot do it with the authority of a speaker actively engaged in the work of legislation. The work of newspapers is really most effective when it consists in enforcing or spreading the views of distinguished public men, — always supposing that such men have the weight and authority they ought to have. The virtual disappearance of these men from our political arena is comparatively recent. If I said that it commenced with the appearance and growth of the machine, I should not be far wrong. There are plenty of men living who in earlier days did not make up their minds about any public question without hearing from Webster, or Clay, or Calhoun, or Silas Wright, or Marcy, or Seward; and they never had to wait very long. These leaders spoke on the question, either in Congress or on the platform, with a distinctness, reasonableness, and thoughtfulness which make their collected speeches, even to-day, very valuable fountains of information and suggestion. I myself can remember the time when the opinion of his party in New York was not fully formed until William H. Seward had said his say; when the business of the newspapers was mainly to comment upon and enforce his views; and when the nearest approach we had to a boss was a devoted follower of an eminent public man, steadily engaged in spreading his fame and pushing his political fortunes.

Now, what is the reason of this change, of the disappearance of this class of men from public life, and of the comparative silence of those we have left? In answering this question I bear in mind the caution I have already expressed against giving only one cause for political effects; but I can myself make no analysis of American political manners which does not prove that the control of all entrance to public life by the boss and the machine is the chief reason why we are cut off from political instruction by people actually engaged in the work of government. There is no term of politics more frequently used than the term "responsibility," but the popular notion of its meaning is very vague. Men in office live under two kinds of responsibility. One is the

theoretical responsibility, under all political constitutions, of officials to the people who elect
them and pay them. But the other, and the one
far more strongly felt, is responsibility to those
from whom they get the permission to contend
for the prizes of public life. These, and not the
people, are their real masters. It is they who
permit them to enter on the public stage; it is
they who can dismiss them or close their political career. The one is a vague, theoretical, or
literary responsibility; the other is real, practical, and constantly present to every office-holder's
mind. The boss and the machine hold the keys
to all our leading offices. It is they who say
whether a man shall even be allowed to compete
for public favor. It is they who decide whether
a second term in office shall be accorded to him,
whether his career in public life shall be closed
or continued. This question, as he knows well,
is determined by considerations which have little
to do with the real value of his public services.
It is determined by secret rules of distribution in
the matter of offices, of which every boss has a
code. Whether the man shall have a nomination depends largely, not on his exposition of
political doctrine or on his advocacy of certain
measures, but on his services as an instrumentality for the division of patronage; for it is with
patronage simply, and but rarely with measures

of policy, that the boss occupies himself. It is
he who decides what kind of office one who
wishes to enter public life shall hold; whether
he shall be a state legislator or congressman, a
superintendent of insurance or the governor of a
state. I have a case in mind where a man of
some ability was ordered by the boss to resign
his seat in Congress in order to become a city
treasurer, and the order was immediately obeyed.
It is to the boss that such a man has to render
an account of his official career. It is the boss
whom he has to please by his votes and speeches.
It is the boss whose dissatisfaction may ruin
him.

This power of the boss, too, is rendered all
the more effective by our custom of insisting
upon the candidate's residence in the particular
district or locality which he seeks to represent.
In France and England all constituencies can
choose their representatives among all the politicians in the kingdom, no matter where they live.
It is thus nearly impossible for the dissatisfaction of one constituency to exclude a man from
political life. If he offends or fails to satisfy
one, he can, if a man of distinction, almost certainly find another. If he quarrels with one
local boss or caucus, some other is generally
glad to take him up. But with us, a quarrel
with the boss of his residence or home is fatal

to a politician's prospects. This residential qualification is the one thing needed to make the
boss's power over him complete.

Thus I am forced to the conclusion that it is
this real responsibility to the boss and the caucus, and not to the public, which accounts for
the disappearance of distinguished men from
public life, and for the decline of instructive
political oratory. The inducement to public
speaking is a desire to affect the opinion of
those who have real power over a man's career.
There are probably few men who would undertake it for the mere purpose of showing that
they have something to say. They speak to increase their influence with the public ; to prove
their fidelity as public servants ; to insure a continuance of public confidence in them, and thus
to insure their continuance in the official positions they occupy. When the public has ceased
to possess any power over their political career,
when their renomination no longer depends upon
public favor, the necessity of conciliating or im-
pressing the public is naturally less felt, if felt
at all. The boss controls every office in the
principal states. He does not unite these offices
in his own person, as Augustus or Tiberius did,
but he designates the persons who are to hold
them, and they accept his dicta with increasing
docility. It is, therefore, not surprising that

the boss's wishes, his idiosyncrasies, his standards of political efficiency and duty, and not those of the public, should be constantly present to the candidate's mind; that he should seek most of all to please the boss. For oratory the boss has no use or admiration. His ideal of a public man is one who votes right, but does not talk, while the public has but little taste for or interest in the man who does not put himself in frequent and interesting communication with it. I dare say there are few in New York to-day who know the names of more than one or two of the Representatives in Congress from the city. The man in office feels but one responsibility; for no man can serve two masters, and the power which gave him his place and can take it away, is the master whom he seeks to serve in the ways the master prefers.

It is hardly necessary to dwell on the effect of this on the tone of public life. But there is one point connected with the making of what is called " tone " which ought not to be passed without mention, and that is the necessity, for its maintenance, of complete publicity as to the reasons for which a man gets office. There is nothing more necessary for the maintenance of what I may call political health than that all the world should know why a certain man gets a certain place. The distribution of place for secret reasons is one of the worst abuses of despotism, and the possibility of its return among us used to be dwelt on with a certain terror by the earlier commentators on the Constitution. Of course, I speak only of the larger and more responsible places concerning which public curiosity is excited. If these are even partially filled by men who do not appear to have reached them by what Burke called "manly arts," — that is, by public services or openly ascertained qualifications, — the effect on tone is very rapid and very marked; for tone consists not more in self-respect than in respect for those with whom one has to act. All attainment of public places by secret favor or intrigue, and the sudden appearance in responsible positions, for reasons unknown to the community, of men of patent unfitness, naturally lowers in their own estimation all the rest of the body to which they belong.

It is hardly within my plan to speak of remedies, and yet no discussion even of the tendencies of our nominating system would be adequate which did not make some attempt to say whether any substitute for it can be provided. I do not conceal my belief that the present system is the great canker of American institutions. I do not believe it can be long practiced without changing the structure of the government. It is accustoming the less intelligent class to what is really a new form, and is reducing the more intelligent to the despair of helplessness; and yet the maintenance intact of any government depends largely on popular habit and confidence. No constitution can retain its vigorous vitality which exists on paper simply; it must also be rooted in popular customs and ideas. The type of statesmanship which a democratic constitution calls for must be carefully preserved, and so must the orthodox sources of distinction. Any growing willingness to be content with inferior men has to be combated; the old ideals must be upheld. But when we come to speak of substitutes, we are met at the outset by the difficulty that the persons to be reformed are in the possession of power, and are thoroughly satisfied with the present system. They predominate in Congress and in most of the legislatures in the country, and would resist vigorously any attempt at change. People seeking something different at their hands would be likely to meet with the same reception as the European democrats who, after the downfall of Napoleon, sought constitutions at the hands of despotic monarchs. The class called the politicians have the strongest interest in the maintenance of the existing state of things. Moreover, the elected convention has effected such a lodgment in our political manners that any attempt at change would possibly be met with a good deal of popular indifference or dislike.

But in considering remedies we have of course to take note of the evils to be remedied. The primary meeting is defective : first, in that the party voters attend it in only very small numbers, and consequently it has ceased to express the party will, or expresses it only very inadequately ; second, in that, as we know it at present, it offers no obstacles to the carrying out of arrangements made secretly and beforehand by the boss or managers. The delegates to be elected are generally decided on before the primary meets, and they are rarely persons who represent the intelligence or morality of the party. Any sufficient remedy, therefore, would either furnish inducements to voters to attend the party primaries, or furnish some substitute for the primaries, or in some way prevent such secret selections as are now made by the boss in advance of the meeting.

Dr. Clarke, of Oswego, who has labored on this question for a great many years, and has produced a plan of reform which he has in vain tried to get embodied in legislation, proposes to overcome the difficulty of popular indolence and indifference by dividing the voters into small district constituencies, of the same size as regards numbers, and drawn by lot from the total number of registered voters. These small constituencies, say of one hundred apiece, are each to choose an electoral delegate, and the assembly of all these delegates is, in a city, to elect the mayor or other elective officers. This is in effect, as far as the size of the constituencies is concerned, really the present system in a rougher shape. Each district is treated as a separate entity, and controlled by "a leader," who generally gets his living by holding some inferior public place, and keeps the voters of his party in discipline and order. The difference comes when Dr. Clarke proceeds to choose the "electoral delegates." The machine insists on designating them beforehand, and prescribing for whom they shall vote in any election in which they may take part. Dr. Clarke would conceal them from the machine by selecting them by lot, like jurymen, and making their services compulsory. The plan, then, has the two great merits of diminishing the size of the constituencies in an orderly manner, and of concealing from the boss the delegates who would be chosen. But the difficulty of its adoption lies not only in the latter fact, but also in the fact that it obscures or hinders the direct action, through party organization, of the free popular will which the masses still fondly believe to be within their reach and which they strongly desire. Its adaptation to our system of government, too, is therefore not so simple.[1]

Another of the great difficulties of party primaries is the difficulty of determining who has a right to vote at them. The present mode of nominating assumes that a man always belongs to the same party, and always votes its ticket under all circumstances. Consequently, the usual qualification for a party voter is having

[1] Dr. Clarke has complained to me that I have done him injustice in this description of his system, and has sent me some further elucidations of it, which I have read carefully. But I am still unable to see where I have gone wrong. I acknowledge freely the very great improvement it would effect in our mode of nominating. I have simply said that the selection of the nominating caucus or convention by lots cast by the whole body of the voters would not satisfy party preferences which are very strong, too strong I admit, among Americans. It might often result in Democrats having to vote for Republicans, or *vice versa*. In other words, it involves the disappearance of party distinctions from elections. "The names of all the voters in a ward are deposited in a panel. They are drawn therefrom by lot in equal companies or lots, say, of 100 each. Each of these lots is a " primary electoral constituency," and chooses "an electoral delegate." The delegates thus chosen meet " and elect the mayor and such other officers of the city at large as are chosen by the people." This would be an excellent system in a city won over to non-partisanship, but it would be impossible to call it to a reform in our nominating system unless it could be used for state and national elections. I have asked Dr. Clarke what provision he makes for party preferences. He answers, " I make none; what I seek is to restore the people to freedom." What I fear is, that the people will insist on provision for party preference in any nominating system, or in other words refuse freedom on Dr. Clarke's terms.

voted the party presidential ticket at the previous election. But he may not have done so, for various reasons that no longer have any force; or he may since then have changed his mind, and may honestly desire to change his party. Party belongings are matters of opinion. We can only know from a man's own statement to which party he really belongs, and it is against public policy to throw obstacles in the way of any citizen's going freely from one party to another. It is through this possibility of change that public opinion acts on government. Yet in our nominating system we treat party as a permanent status, the loss of which excludes a man from all share in the work of nomination. For instance, unless I voted for Blaine in 1884 I could not participate in the selection of Harrison in 1888, and unless I voted for Cleveland in 1888 I should have been incompetent to aid in selecting him as the party candidate in 1892. So that in devising any reform, the existence and utility of parties have to be acknowledged, and means have to be provided for recognizing a genuine party man and for the protection of primary meetings or conventions against bogus voters. I have not heard of any such practical available test, and the invention of one, as long as people insist on government through party, will be difficult.

The only mode of escape from this difficulty as yet devised is what is called "independent voting;" that is, refusal to belong to any party, and free passage from one to another, as the circumstances may seem to require. But this necessarily involves the abandonment of any share in the work of selecting party candidates, and shuts the voter up to choice between two on whose nomination he has had no influence. Moreover, it takes out of each party, if it is to be effective, a large body of the most thoughtful and patriotic of the voters; that is, of persons who still retain a keen sense of the fact that party is an instrument, not an end, and whose aid would be most valuable in raising the character of nominations. I do not think I err in saying that the power of the machine and of the boss over nominations has increased *pari passu* with the growth of independent voting. Each party, in getting rid of its more mutinous or recalcitrant members, solidifies the power of the machine, makes insurrection less frequent, and renders "kicking," as it is called, more odious. It weeds out of the party management, too, the element most sensitive to public opinion, and most anxious to secure the approbation of the more thoughtful class of the community. What remains is composed of men hardened against criticism, indifferent to all approbation or dis-

approbation but that of their own fellows, and
knowing little of any political virtue except that
of fidelity to party friends.   In the State of
New York, which may be said to be the arena
in which all political tendencies first show themselves, this has been strikingly true.   In no
other state is the independent vote so powerful
and active as in New York, and in none is the
machine so audacious or so insensible to warning.   The overthrow of one party by this vote
seems only to suggest imitation to the other.
Each follows closely the very ways which have
brought ruin on its predecessor, so that the
independent vote is brought almost to the end
of its resources.   It can punish one party only
by putting the other in power, but this party
takes care that the condition of things which
brought on the punishment shall continue un-
changed, and even finds means to negotiate with
the other for a division of patronage.

"Independent voting" then has clearly ceased
to be a remedy.   Something better has still to
be found.   The most popular remedy is throwing the protection of law around the caucus or
primary meeting, and making frauds in its composition, or in the conduct of the proceedings,
criminal offenses.   This, it is true, would prevent such cheating as took place in New York
in 1895, but it would not secure a larger attend-

ance of the voters, which is the chief need of the primary meeting. The meeting would still fail to represent the bulk of the party, though the law might make those who were present more decorous. And as assuredly as the attendance continued to be small, it would be controlled and its proceedings be prearranged by those who had personal interest in being present. Legalization would not overcome the reluctance of indolent or busy voters to take part in a proceeding which was not conclusive, and in which any opposition to a programme previously arranged by active party managers would make them unpopular, and expose them to discussions to which they would feel unequal. It would prevent gross frauds on the spot and make attendance safe and orderly, but it would do nothing towards making the primary a full representative of party opinion and feeling. In other words, it would still continue to grind out results carefully prepared by the boss, and the art of politics would continue to be taught to our youth, not as the art of government, but as the art of " getting delegates."

Is the situation then hopeless? Are we tied up inexorably simply to a choice of evils? I think not. It seems to me that the nomination of candidates is another of the problems of democracy which are never seriously attacked without prolonged perception and discussion of their importance. One of these was the formation of the federal government; another was the abolition of slavery; another was the reform of the civil service. Every one of them looked hopeless in the beginning; but the solution came, in each case, through the popular determination to find some better way. In all ages this has been one of the democratic characteristics. It is the only régime in which there is no disposition to stagnate. It may improve or it may deteriorate, but it is an incessant movement, and has a passion for experiments, some of which end badly, but those which have behind them the general human instinctive longing for efficiency are apt to succeed in the end.

Since the foregoing observations were written, an attempt at a remedy has been made in New York, which has met with a very encouraging measure of success. The supporters of Mr. Low, the independent candidate for the mayoralty of the "Greater New York," having broken loose from all party organizations, determined on trying the plan of nomination by petition, that is of procuring in each district of the city the legally requisite number of signatures of voters to a petition requesting Mr. Low to become a candidate. Mr. Low's compliance was followed by a highly instructive canvass, because it was necessarily free from irrelevant matter, such as appeals to party loyalty, or warnings of the bad effect of party defeat on other than municipal matters. All the speeches made and documents issued necessarily bore on the issues raised by the contest for the mayoralty. The condition of the city government, its causes and remedies, were almost the only matters discussed. The candidate, having no party support to rely on, or party preferences to appeal to, was compelled to appear personally on the stump, and make good his own claims to the place. The campaign was, in fact, in the best sense " educational." It was violently opposed by a large body of voters who professed to have the same aims in the affairs of the city, on the ground of want of " regularity," that is, a departure from party rules and precedents, or in other words, of disregard of the caucus system of nomination. But the result was a vote of 151,000 in a total of 526,000, or nearly one third. As a first attempt at a better way, this must be considered very encouraging. It has shown clearly that the caucus, in cities at least, is not necessary, and thus has got rid of the idea, which in cities is the greatest obstacle to the discovery of a remedy, that for purposes of nomination there must be a meeting, in a certain place, at a certain time. Nearly all efforts now being made, or

which have been made to " reform the primary,"
assume this necessity.   They all arrange for an
assemblage of some sort.   But a primary in a
city or large town consists of a number of
people unknown to each other, of various classes
and conditions and of various ages, and is almost certain to be managed by those who make
it a business to attend to " politics," and therefore, like all meetings, is sure to be confronted
by a preconcerted programme prepared by those
who are most interested in the result.   Opposition to this programme is something which most
voters will be unwilling to undertake publicly,
either through timidity, or want of practice in
public speaking, or ignorance of the facts.
They will therefore either remain silent, or
more probably remain at home and allow the
plan of the managers to be carried out without
opposition, so that no matter how many guarantees the law may provide for the orderliness or
fairness of a primary, it is sure, in cities or large
centres of population, to fall into the hands of
the professional politicians.   Other classes will
cease to attend, for the simple reason that they
will find the result determined on before they
reach the place.   Therefore, it is to be feared
that no matter how often we reform the primary,
the non-appearance of the better class of voters
is pretty sure, in the end, to leave the work of
nomination in the same hands as before.

THE DECLINE OF LEGISLATURES

I

THE Roman Senate was the prototype of all modern legislatures. It had two great functions, *auctoritas* and *consilium*. The former was practically what we call the " veto; " that is, the Senate could forbid any legislation not originating with itself, whether proposed by the people in the *comitia* or by the magistrates. Nothing became a law without its sanction. The latter, *consilium*, was nearly what we call " advice and consent; " that is, the Senate had to pass on all proposals submitted to it by the executive officers, and approve or amend, as the case might be. In considering the proposals of the people, it decided whether they were wise and Roman ; but it consulted with the magistrates concerning every important action or enterprise about to be undertaken. In all this it acted under two powerful restraints, partly like the theocracy in the early days of New England, partly like our constitutions to-day, — namely, the *mos majorum* and the auguries. It saw that everything was done in the Roman or

ancient way, and that the unseen forces were
likely to favor it.[1]   Now, how did this system
succeed?   On this point I cannot do better than
quote the testimony of Mommsen : —

"Nevertheless, if any revolution or any usurpation appears justified before the bar of history
by exclusive ability to govern, even its rigorous
judgment must acknowledge that this corporation duly comprehended and worthily fulfilled
its great task.   Called to power, not by the
empty accident of birth, but substantially by the
free choice of the nation ; confirmed every fifth
year by the stern moral judgment of the wor-
thiest men ; holding office for life, and so not
dependent on the expiration of its commission or
on the varying opinion of the people ; having its
ranks close and united even after the equaliza-
tion of its orders ; embracing in it all the political intelligence and practical statesmanship that
the people possessed ; absolute in dealing with
all financial questions and in the control of foreign policy ; having complete power over the
executive by virtue of its brief duration and of
the tribunitian intercession which was at the service of the Senate after the termination of the
quarrels between the orders, — the Roman Senate was the noblest organ of the nation, and in
consistency and political sagacity, in unanimity

[1] Willems' *Sénat et République Romaine*, pp. 34, 35.

and patriotism, in grasp of power and unwavering courage, the foremost political corporation of all times; still even now an 'Assembly of Kings,' which knew well how to combine despotic energy with republican self-devotion." [1]

As I have said, the Senate was the prototype of all modern legislatures; but only two, since the fall of the Roman Empire, have at all resembled it, the Venetian Grand Council and the British Parliament.   No others in the modern world have attempted to discharge so great a variety of duties, such as holding large extents of conquered territory and ruling great bodies of subject population, or carrying on foreign wars. Its chief distinction was that, as a rule, subjects for consideration, on which it had to take positive action, did not originate with it, but were brought before it by the executive officers engaged in the active conduct of the government. So that it may be called a consultative rather than a legislative body.   How this came about and how it continued, it is not necessary to discuss here.   The general result was that, through the whole course of Roman history, the administrative officers remained actually in charge of the government, subject to the advice and control of the legislature.   The same system has prevailed in the British Parliament ever since it

[1] *History of Rome,* vol. i. pp. 410–412.

became a real power in the state. Its proceedings are controlled and regulated by the executive officers. They submit measures to it, and ask its advice and consent; but if they cannot carry them, the matter drops and they resign, and others undertake the task. Practically, a private member cannot originate a bill, or get it discussed, or procure its passage, except with their consent. Indeed, as a legislator he is always in a certain sense an intruder. The function of the two Houses is essentially, not the drafting or proposing of laws, but seeing that no law is passed which is not expedient and " constitutional ; " " constitutional " being, in the British sense, what the Romans meant by being in accordance with the *mos majorum* and having the approval of the auguries. The British ministry, in fact, legislates as well as administers. Every bill is fathered by the man who is engaged in the active work of the department which it touches. If it relate to the finances, it is framed and introduced by the Chancellor of the Exchequer; if it relate to shipping, by the President of the Board of Trade; if to the army, by the Secretary of War, and so on. Any private member who should attempt to regulate these things would be frowned down and silenced. His business is to hear what the ministry proposes, and to pass judgment on it.

The reason why the English have been able to preserve what is called the " cabinet system " in their proceedings — that is, the dominance of the executive officers in the deliberation of Parliament — is, I need hardly say, historical. Parliaments may be said to have originated as a check on the royal authority. In the House of Commons government was represented by the king. The ministry was emphatically his ministry; the opposition was held together partly by fear, and partly by dislike of him. It never reached the point of seeking to take the administration of the government out of his hands or out of those of his officers, except in the rebellion of 1640. Its highest ambition was to be consulted about what was going to be done, and to be allowed to ask questions about it and to vote the money for it. It never thought of taking on itself the function of administration. It confined itself to the exercise of a veto. The ministry never parted with its power of initiation, and it strengthened its position by what may be called the solidarity of the cabinet; that is, the practice of treating each act of any particular minister as the act of the whole body, and standing or falling by it as such. The occasions have been rare, in English history, in which any one member has been surrendered to the dissatisfaction or reprobation of the opposition. When Puritan and Cavalier were succeeded by Whig and Tory, or Whig and Tory by Conservative and Liberal, the new order merely substituted one executive for another in the House of Commons, and did not create a new kind of executive. No matter what the relative strength of parties in the country might be, the dominant party appeared in the House of Commons simply as administrative officers, seeking and taking advice and approval from the representative body.

Now, the value of the preservation of the consultative rather than the legislative function by the House of Commons, the *auctoritas* and *consilium* rather than the initiative, has been brought out more clearly than ever by the history of legislative bodies on the Continent since the revival of popular government in 1848, and by the history of legislatures in this country since the war. The English House of Commons, one may say, has grown up under the consultative system. No other system has ever been seen or thought of. Private members have learnt to sit and listen, to have their opinions asked for on certain proposals, and, if their advice is not taken, to seek their remedy in choosing other agents. They act on all proposals submitted by the ministry, in parties, not singly. The experience of three centuries has taught each member to be of the same mind, in every case, as those with whom he ordinarily agrees on other subjects. When the House of Commons was taken as a model on the Continent, especially after 1848, what was set up was not really the English Parliament, but a set of councils for discussion, in which every man had the right of initiative, or, at all events, the right to say his say without sharing with any one else the responsibility for what he said. The new governments all had ministries, after the English fashion, but no one in the legislature felt bound to approve, or felt bound to join others in disapproving, of their policy. In other words, the cabinet system did not take root in the political manners. In his Journals, during a visit to Turin in 1850, Senior records a conversation with Cesare Balbo, a member of the Chamber in the first Piedmontese Parliament, in which Balbo said, after an exciting financial debate : " We have not yet acquired parliamentary discipline. Most of the members are more anxious about their own crotchets or their own consistency than about the country. The ministry has a large nominal majority, but every member of it is ready to put them in a minority for any whim of his own." [1] This was probably true of every legislative body on the Continent, and

[1] Senior's *Journals*, vol. i. p. 323.

it continues true to this day in Italy, Greece, France, Austria, Germany, and the new Australian democracies.

Parliamentary discipline has not gained in strength. On the contrary, the tendency to give new men a taste of parliamentary life, which is very strong particularly in France and Italy, has stimulated the disposition to form " groups," or to act independently. A man who is likely to serve for only one term is unwilling to sink himself either in the ministerial majority, or in the opposition. He wishes to make a reputation for himself, and this he cannot do by voting silently under a chief. A reputation has to be made by openly expressed criticism, or by open hostility, or by the individual exercise of the initiative. To make an impression on his constituents, he has to have a programme of his own and to push it, to identify himself with some cause which the men in power either ignore, or treat too coolly. As a rule, the Continental legislatures, while modeled on the British or cabinet system, have really not copied its most important feature, the dominance of the executive in the legislative body. In Austria and Germany, where the king or emperor is still a power, this is not so apparent, but in France and Italy and in Australia, where the Parliament is well-nigh omnipotent, the result is incessant changes of ministry, and a great deal of legislation, intended not so much to benefit the country as to gather up and hold a majority.

In America we have never tried the cabinet system, partly because our legislatures were started before this system became fairly established in England, and partly because, in colonial times, the executive was never in thoroughly friendly relations with the legislative department of any colony. Americans entered on their national existence with the only sort of legislature that was then known, a council of equals, where one man had as much right to originate legislation as another, subject, of course, to the general policy of the party to which he belonged. The device with which we have striven to meet the confusion thus created, is the formation of committees to examine and report upon every project of law submitted by individual members. Every legislature, including Congress, is now divided into these committees. With the executive it has no open or official relations, for purposes of discussion. No administrative officer is entitled of right to address, or advise, or consult it. He is exposed to constant criticism, but he cannot explain or answer. His presence, even, in the legislative chambers is an intrusion. He can communicate in writing any information which the legislature demands, but this is the

limit of his relations with it.   The President
and every Governor of a state have the right to
send what we call " messages " to the legislature, directing its attention to certain matters
and recommending certain action, but it is very
rare for these recommendations to have much
effect.   The messages are rhetorical perform-
ances, intended to give the public an idea of
the capacity and opinions of the writers rather
than to furnish a foundation for law-making.

There is nothing more striking in our system
than the perfunctoriness which has overtaken
both these documents and the party platforms,
and there can be no better illustration of the
effect of the absence of the executive from the
legislative chambers.   If there were a ministry,
or if there were members of a cabinet sitting in
the chambers and charged with the initiation of
legislation, they would naturally be charged also
with the duty of carrying out the President's or
the Governor's recommendations, and embodying
the party platform in laws.   But under the committee system nobody is burdened with this duty,
and after the messages and platforms have been
printed, they do not often receive any further
attention.   Few can remember what a party platform contains, a month after its adoption, and it
is very seldom that any legislative notice is taken
of it, except by the opposition press, which occa-

sionally uses it to twit the party in power with
its inconsistency or negligence.   In fact, legislation, both in Congress and in the state legislatures, may be said to have become government by
committee.   The individual member has hardly
more to do with it than he has in England.   Yet
this does not prevent his making attempts to
legislate.   He does not ask permission to introduce bills, but he introduces them by thousands
every session.   His right to legislate is recognized as good and valid, but the rules which
regulate the course of his bill through the House
make the right of little more value than that of
the private member of the House of Commons.
His bill, as soon as it is presented, passes into
the custody of one of the committees.   He is not
allowed to say a word in its behalf, and he has
no knowledge of what its fate will be.   He is
literally cut off from debate, no less by the rules
than by the Speaker's favor.   This functionary,
by simply refusing to see him, can condemn him
to perpetual silence, and has no hesitation in
exercising his power to advance or retard such
business of the House as he approves or dislikes.

But there is this difference between the position of the English and that of the American
member.   In England, the persons who take
his bill out of his hands, or refuse him permission to introduce it, are themselves engaged in

the work of legislation. They are responsible for the conduct of the government. They profess to be supplying all the legislation that is necessary. They simply deny the private member any participation in their work. In America, the committee which takes his bill from him and seals its fate is composed of his own equals. They have no more to do with the executive than he has. They are no more charged with legislation on any particular subject than he is. Their main function is to examine and "report," but whether they will ever report is a matter entirely within their discretion. They are not bound to substitute anything for what they reject or ignore. They have so much to pass upon, that their duty of initiation is reduced to a minimum. Moreover, when they report favorably on any bill in their custody, or originate one of their own, they are not bound to allow full discussion of it in the open House. All needful discussion of it is supposed to have taken place in their chamber. If any one is allowed to say much about it in the House, it is rather as a matter of grace; and unless he is an orator of reputation, but few listen to him. Consequently, there is in practice a wide difference between the control of legislation in the British Parliament, and the control in our Congress. With us it is exercised by an entirely different class of persons, who are not accountable for the fate of any bill. If they choose not to report it, they are not bound to give their reasons. The function of the British ministry is to provide the necessary legislation, and as a rule, the ministry is composed of men well known to the public and of more than usual experience. The function of the American committee, on the other hand, is simply to sift or impede the efforts of a large assembly, composed of persons of equal authority, to pass laws, with the execution of which, if they were passed, they would have nothing to do. As everybody has a right to introduce bills, without being in any way responsible for their working, there must be some power to examine, revise, choose, or reject, and this need is supplied by the committee system.[1]

The great change in the position and powers of the Speaker in Congress and in all American legislatures has been due to the same causes as the institution of the committees. He has been changed from his prototype, the judicial officer who presides over debates in the House of Commons, into something like the European prime minister, so that he has charge of the legislation

[1] The working of this system and the actual functions of the Speaker are well described in Wilson's *Congressional Government*, and in Miss Follett's *Speaker of the House of Representatives*.

of his party. He appoints the various committees, and can in this way make himself feared
or courted by members. By his power of "recognition" he can consign any member to obscurity. He can encourage or hinder a committee
in any species of legislation. He can check or
promote extravagance. He makes no pretension
to impartiality; he professes simply to be as impartial as a man can be who has to look after
the interests of his own party and see that its
"policy" is carried out. In fact, he differs but
little from the "leader" of the House of Commons, except that he has nothing to do with the
execution of the laws after he has helped to
make them. He may have to hand them over
to a hostile Senate or to a hostile executive, after
he has secured their passage in his own assembly,
and the country does not hold him responsible
for them. No matter how badly they may work,
the blame is laid, not on him, but on "the
House" or on the party. He has nothing personal to fear from their failure, however active
he may have been in securing their enactment.
But the steady acquiescence in his increased
assumption of power in every session of Congress
or of the legislatures is clearly an admission that
modern democratic legislatures need leaders.

There are two committees which may be said
to be charged with the work of legislation, and

these are the Committee of Ways and Means
and the Committee on Appropriations. But
neither of them supplies what may be called a
"budget;" that is, a statement of necessary expenditure and of probable revenue. These cal-
culations are made, it is true, in the various
administrative offices, but the committees are not
bound to take notice of them. The Committee
of Ways and Means fixes the revenue, as a rule,
mainly with regard to the state of public opinion
touching the principal source of revenue, the
taxes on imports. If the public is deemed to be
at that moment favorable to protection, these
taxes are put high; if favorable to free trade,
they are put low. The relation to the public
outlay is not made the chief consideration. In
other words, "taxation for revenue only" is not
an art practiced by either party. Taxation is
avowedly practiced as the art of encouraging
domestic industry in some degree. The Committee on Appropriations has no relations with
the Ways and Means Committee. It does not
concern itself about income. It adds to the
necessary expenditure of the government such
further expenditure as is likely to be popular, as
that for river and harbor improvements and for
pensions. In this way, neither committee is responsible for a deficit, for neither is bound to
make ends meets.

This absence of connection between the levying and the spending authorities would work
speedy ruin in any European government. The
danger or inconvenience of it here has been con-
cealed by the very rapid growth of the country
in wealth and population, and the resulting rapid
increase of the revenue under all circumstances.
It is not too much to say that the first serious
deficiency of revenue was experienced on the
outbreak of the civil war. After the war, there
was no difficulty in meeting all reasonable expenses, until the yearly recurring and increasing
surplus bred a frame of mind about expenditure
which led to enormous appropriations for pensions and domestic improvements. These have
at last brought about, and for the first time in
American history, a real difficulty in devising
sources of revenue. At this writing the question under debate is what taxes will be most
popular in the country, when it ought to be
what taxes will bring in most income. This has
been largely due to the appropriations for purposes not absolutely necessary, but the Committee of Ways and Means is compelled to treat
them as if they were legitimate expenses. This
separation between the power which lays taxes
and the power which spends them is probably
the boldest of our experiments, and one which
has never before been tried. Its inconveniences

are likely to be felt increasingly, as the habits bred by easy circumstances become more fixed.

The tendency to lavish expenditure has been stimulated, too, by he temptation of the protective system to make a large revenue collected from duties on imports seem necessary. All governments are prone to make taxation serve some other purpose than to raise revenue; that is, to foster or maintain some sort of polity. It was used for ages to promote inequality; now it is frequently used to promote certain special interests. In England, the import duties on corn were meant to benefit the landed interest and foster large estates. In America, the duties on imports are meant to benefit native manufactures indirectly; but by showing that they are also essential to the government, a great deal of the opposition to them as a benefit to the manufacturers is disarmed. In no way can the needs of the government be made so conspicuous as by keeping the treasury empty. Since protection for industry was, after the war, incorporated in the fiscal system of the government, therefore it has begotten extravagance almost as an inevitable accompaniment. The less money there is on hand, the higher does it seem that duties ought to be; and the way to keep little on hand is to spend freely.

The difficulty of getting rid of the protective

system, in any modern country, is to be found in part in the growth of democracy. To the natural man, protection for his products against competition is one of the primary duties of government. Every citizen or mechanic would fain keep the neighboring market to himself, if he could. The shoemaker wishes to make all the shoes of his village, the carpenter to do all the carpentering. In fact, protection is the economical creed which the "uninstructed political economist" always lays hold of first. Its benefits seem clearest, and its operation in his own interest is most visible and direct. This undoubtedly goes far to account for the failure of the free-trade theory to make more way in the world since the days of its early apostles. The arguments by which it is supported are a little too abstract and complex for the popular mind. The consequence is that a distinct revival of protectionism has accompanied the spread of popular government in Europe and Australia, as well as in this country. The use of the government to keep the market for his products, and the theory that the market is a privilege for the seller which he ought not to be expected to share with an alien, will long meet with ready acceptance from the workingman. Whatever be its industrial or economical merits or demerits, its effect politically, in stimulating expenditure

in the United States, has been plain; and as
long as taxpayers respond so readily to pecuniary demands on them as they have always hitherto done, close calculation of outgoings and
incomings will not be easy to bring about. At
present, the " elasticity " of our revenue, owing
to the rapid increase of our population and the
magnitude of our undeveloped resources, is one
of the great wonders of European financiers, and
renders the education of financial experts difficult. Any source of taxation which even the
most inexperienced of our economists reaches, is
apt to pour forth results so abundantly as to
make the caution, the anxiety, and the nice
adjustments on which the financial system of
the Old World is based, appear unnecessary or
even ridiculous.

But the most serious defect in the committee
system, and the one that is hardest to remedy, is
the stopper it puts on debate. The objection is
often made, and with a show of reason, to the
cabinet system, and its practice of deciding
things only after open discussion, that it unduly stimulates mere talk, and postpones actual
business for the purpose of allowing a large
number of persons to produce arguments which
are found not to be worth listening to, and
which have no real influence on the results.
This is true, in particular, of all countries in

which, as on the Continent, an attempt has been
made to govern assemblies without parliamentary
discipline, and without practice in acting by parties rather than singly or in groups.   Various
forms of " closure " have been invented in order
to check this habit.   It may be found in an
extreme degree in our own Senate, which has
no closure, and in which irrelevant speeches are
inflicted by the hour, and even by the day, on
unwilling listeners.

But our demand on legislative bodies for
" business " has carried us to the other extreme,
which may be seen in the House of Representatives.   There is nothing, after all, more important to the modern world than that the intelligence and character of the nation should find
their way into the legislatures ; and for this
purpose the legislatures should be made something more than scenes of obscurity, hard work,
and small pay.   The English House of Commons
owed its attractiveness for two centuries, in spite
of the non-payment of members, to the fact that
it was " the pleasantest club in Europe."   It was
also a place in which any member, however humble his beginnings, had a chance to make fame
as an orator.   In recent days, legislatures in all
the democratic countries have been made repulsive to men of mark by the pains taken " to get
business done" and to keep down the flood of

speech. Everybody who enters a legislature now for the first time, especially if he is a man of talent and character, is bitterly disappointed by finding that the rules take from him nearly every opportunity of distinction, and, in addition, condemn him to a great deal of obscure drudgery. It is only by the rarest chance that he finds an opening to speak, and his work on the committees never shows itself to the public. It consists largely in passing on the merits of the thousands of schemes concocted by inexperienced or ignorant men, and has really some resemblance to a college professor's reading of "themes." In fact, the committee room may be called the grave of honorable ambition.

We find, accordingly, that only few men of real capacity, who have once gone to the legislature or to Congress, are willing to return for a second term, simply because they find the work disagreeable and the reward inadequate; for it is one of the commonplaces of politics that, in every country, the number of able men who will serve the public without either pay or distinction is very small. Even the most patriotic must have one or the other; and to set up legislatures, as all the democratic countries have done, in which no one can look for either, is an experiment fraught with danger. If I am not greatly mistaken, the natural result is beginning

to show itself.   There is not a country in the
world, living under parliamentary government,
which has not begun to complain of the decline
in the quality of its legislators.   More and more,
it is said, the work of government is falling
into the hands of men to whom even small pay
is important, and who are suspected of adding
to their income by corruption.   The withdrawal
of the more intelligent class from legislative duties is more and more lamented, and the com-
plaint is somewhat justified by the mass of crude,
hasty, incoherent, and unnecessary laws which
are poured on the world at every session.   It is
increasingly difficult to-day to get a man of
serious knowledge on any subject to go to Congress, if he have other pursuits and other sources
of income.   To get him to go to the state legislature, in any of the populous and busy states, is
well-nigh impossible.   If he has tried the experiment once, and is unwilling to repeat it, and
you ask him why, he will answer that the secret
committee work was repulsive ; that the silence
and the inability to accomplish anything, imposed on him by the rules, were disheartening ;
and that the difficulty of communicating with
his constituents, or with the nation at large,
through the spoken and reported word, deprived
him of all prospects of being rewarded by celeb-
rity.

It is into the vacancies thus left that the boss steps with full hands. He summons from every quarter needy young men, and helps them to get into places where they will be able to add to their pay by some sort of corruption, however disguised, — perhaps rarely direct bribery, but too often blackmail or a share in jobs. To such it is not necessary that the legislature should be an agreeable place, so long as it promises a livelihood. This system is already working actively in some states; it is spreading to others, and is most perceptible in the great centres of affairs. It is an abuse, too, which in a measure creates what it feeds upon. The more legislatures are filled with bad characters, the less inducement there is for men of a superior order to enter them; for it is true of every sort of public service, from the army up to the cabinet, that men are influenced as to entering it by the kind of company they will have to keep. The statesman will not associate with the Boy, if he can help it, especially in a work in which conference and persuasion play a large part.

If it be true that the character and competency of legislators are declining, the evil is rendered all the more serious by the fact that the general wealth has increased enormously within the present century. Down to the French Revolution, and we might almost say down to 1848,

the western world, speaking broadly, was ruled
by the landholding or rich class.   Its wealth
consisted mainly of land, and the owners of the
land carried on the government.   In commercial
communities, like Genoa or Venice, or the Hanse
Towns, the governing class was made up of
merchants, but it was still the rich class.   Within
fifty years a great change has occurred.   The
improvement in communication has brought all
the land of the world into the great markets,
and as a result the landowners have ceased to be
the wealthy, and the democratic movement has
taken the government away from them.   From
the hands of the wealthy, the power has passed
or is passing into the hands of men to whom the
salary of a legislator is an object of some consequence, and who are more careful to keep in
touch with their constituents than to afford examples of scientific government, even if they
were capable of it.   It cannot be said, in the
light of history, that the new men are giving
communities worse government than they used to
have, but government in their hands is not pro-
gressing in the same ratio as the other arts of
civilization, while the complexity of the interests
to be dealt with is steadily increasing.   Science
and literature are making, and have made, much
more conspicuous advances than the management of common affairs.   Less attention is given

to experience than formerly, while the expectation of some new idea, in which the peculiarities of human nature will have much slighter play, is becoming deeper and more widespread.

No effect of this passage of legislative work into less instructed hands is more curious than the great stimulus it has given to legislation itself. Legislators now, apparently, would fain have the field of legislation as wide as it was in the Middle Ages. The schemes for the regulation of life by law, which are daily submitted to the committees by aspiring reformers, are innumerable. One legislator in Kansas was seeking in the winter of 1896 to procure the enactment of the Ten Commandments. In Nebraska, another has sought to legislate against the wearing of corsets by women. Constant efforts are made to limit the prices of things, to impose fresh duties on common carriers, to restrain the growth of wealth, to promote patriotic feeling by greater use of symbols, or in some manner to improve public morals by artificial restraints. There is no legislature in America which does not contain members anxious to right some kind of wrong, or afford some sort of aid to human character, by a bill. Sometimes the bill is introduced to oblige a constituent, in full confidence that it will never leave the committee room; at others, to rectify some abuse which happens to

have come under the legislator's eye. Sometimes, again, the greater activity of one member
drives into legislation another who had previously looked forward to a silent session. Then
it has to be borne in mind that, under the committee system, which has been faithfully copied
from Congress in all the legislatures, the only
way in which a member can make his constituents aware that he is trying to earn his salary, is
by introducing bills. It does not much matter
that they are not finished pieces of legislation,
or that there is but little chance of their passage.
Their main object is to convince the district that
its representative is awake and active, and has an
eye to its interests. The practice of " log-roll-
ing," too, has become a fixed feature in the procedure of nearly all the legislatures; that is, of
making one member's support of another member's bill conditional on his receiving the other
member's support for his own. In the attempted
revolt against the boss, during the recent senatorial election in New York, a good many members who avowed their sense of Platt's unfitness
for the Senate acknowledged that they could
not vote against him openly, because this would
cause the defeat of local measures in which they
were interested. This recalls the fact that many
even of the best men go to the legislature for
one or two terms, not so much to serve the

public as to secure the passage of bills in which they, or the voters of their district, have a special concern. Their anxiety about these makes their subserviency to the majority complete, on larger questions, however it is controlled. You vote for an obviously unfit man for Senator, for instance, because you cannot risk the success of a bill for putting up a building, or erecting a bridge, or opening a new street, in your own town. You must give and take. These men are reinforced by a large number by whom the service is rendered for simple livelihood. The spoils doctrine — that public office is a prize, or a "plum," rather than a public trust — has effected a considerable lodgment in legislation. Not all receive their places as the Massachusetts farmer received his membership in the legislature, a few years ago, because he had lost some cows by lightning, but a formidable number — young lawyers, farmers carrying heavy mortgages, men without regular occupation and temporarily out of a job — find service in the legislature, even for one term, an attractive mode of tiding over the winter.

The mass of legislation or attempts at legislation due to this state of affairs is something startling. I have been unable to obtain records of the acts and resolutions of all the States for the same year. I am obliged to take those of

Arkansas for the year 1893, four other states for 1894, ten for 1896, and the rest for 1895. But I have taken only one year for each state. The total of such acts and resolutions is 15,730, and this is for a population of 70,000,000. In addition, Congress in 1895–96 passed 457 acts and resolutions. But the amount of work turned out is really not very surprising, when we consider the number of the legislators. There are no less than 447 national legislators and 6578 state legislators, — in all 7025, exclusive of county, city, and all other local authorities capable of passing rules or ordinances. At this ratio of legislators to population, 4000 at least would be engaged on the laws of Great Britain, without any provision for India and the colonies, 3800 on those of France, about 5000 on those of Germany, and 3000 on those of Italy. It will be easily seen what a draft this is on the small amount of legislative capacity which every community contains. There is no country which has yet shown itself capable of producing more than one small first-class legislative assembly. We undertake to keep going forty-five for the states alone, besides those for territories. All these assemblies, too, have to do with interests of the highest order. As a general rule, in all governments, the chief legislative body only is intrusted with the highest functions. Its jurisdiction

covers the weightiest interests of the people who
live under it. The protection of life and property, the administration of civil and criminal
justice, and the imposition of the taxes most
severely felt, are among its duties. All minor
bodies exist as its subordinates or agents, and
exercise only such powers as it is pleased to delegate to them. This draws to the superior assembly, as a matter of course, the leading men
of the country, and by far the larger share of
popular attention.

In the formation of our federal Constitution,
this division, based on relative importance to the
community, was not possible. The states surrendered as little as they could. The federal
government took what it could get, and only
what seemed absolutely necessary to the creation
of a nation. The consequence is that, though
Congress appears to be the superior body, it is
not really so. It is more conspicuous, and, if I
may use the word, more picturesque, but it does
not deal with a larger number of serious public
interests. The states have reserved to themselves the things which most concern a man's
comfort and security as a citizen. The protection of his property, the administration of civil
and criminal justice, the interpretation of con-
tracts and wills, and the creation and regulation
of municipalities, are all within their jurisdic-

tion. Most of the inhabitants pass their lives
without once coming into contact with federal
authority. As a result, an election to Congress
is only seeming political promotion. It gives
the candidate more dignity and importance, but
he really has less to do with the every-day happiness of his fellow citizens than the state legislator. If he were deprived of the power of
raising and lowering the duties on foreign imports and of bickering with foreign powers, his
influence on the daily life of Americans would
be comparatively small. When he goes to
Washington, he finds himself in a larger and
more splendid sphere, but charged with less of
important governmental work. The grave political functions of the country are discharged in
the state legislatures, but by inferior men. In
so far as Congress makes a draft on the legislative capacity of the nation, it makes it at the
expense of the local governments.

For this anomaly it would be difficult to suggest a remedy. The division of powers between
the confederation and the states, though not a
logical one, was probably the only possible one
at the time it was made. The main work of government was left to the states, but the field at
Washington was made by its conspicuousness
more attractive to men of talent and energy in
politics; so that it may be said that we give an

inordinate share of our parliamentary ability to affairs which concern us in only a minor degree. This, however, can hardly be considered as the result of a democratic tendency. The federal arrangement has really nothing to do with democracy. It was made as the only practicable mode of bringing several communities into peaceful relations, and enabling them to face the world as a nation, though it might as readily have been the work of aristocracies as of democracies; but in so far as it has in any degree lowered the character of legislative bodies, democracy has been made and will be made to bear the blame.

This opinion has been strengthened by the discredit which has overtaken two very prominent features of the federal arrangement, — the election of the President by the electoral college and the election of Senators by the state legislatures. The fact is that the complete disuse of their electoral functions within forty years after the adoption of the Constitution was one of the most striking illustrations that history affords of the futility of political prophecy. Here is the judgment on this feature of their work by the framers of the Constitution, as set forth in "The Federalist : " —

" As the select assemblies for choosing the President, as well as the state legislatures who

appoint the Senators, will in general be composed
of the most enlightened and respectable citizens,
there is reason to presume that their attention
and their votes will be directed to those men
only who have become the most distinguished by
their abilities and virtue, and in whom the people perceive just grounds for confidence. The
Constitution manifests very particular attention
to this object. By excluding men under thirty-
five from the first office, and those under thirty
from the second, it confines the electors to men
of whom the people have had time to form a
judgment, and with respect to whom they will
not be liable to be deceived by those brilliant
appearances of genius and patriotism which, like
transient meteors, sometimes mislead as well as
dazzle. If the observation be well founded, that
wise kings will always be served by able ministers, it is fair to argue that as an assembly of
select electors possess, in a greater degree than
kings, the means of extensive and accurate information relative to men and characters, so will
their appointments bear at least equal marks of
discretion and discernment. The inference is
that President and Senators so chosen will always
be of the number of those who best understand
our national interests, whether considered in relation to the several states or to foreign nations,
who are best able to promote those interests, and

whose reputation for integrity inspires and merits confidence. With such men the power of making treaties may be safely lodged." [1]

And here is the opinion of the earliest and most philosophic of our foreign observers, M. de Tocqueville : —

"When you enter the House of Representatives at Washington, you are struck with the vulgar aspect of this great assembly. The eye looks often in vain for a celebrated man. Nearly all its members are obscure personages, whose names suggest nothing to the mind. They are for the most part village lawyers, dealers, or even men belonging to the lowest classes. In a country in which education is almost universal, it is said there are representatives of the people who cannot always write correctly. Two steps away opens the hall of the Senate, whose narrow area incloses a large part of the celebrities of America. One hardly sees there a single man who does not recall the idea of recent fame. They are eloquent advocates, or distinguished generals, or able magistrates, or well-known statesmen. Every word uttered in this great assembly would do honor to the greatest parliamentary debates in Europe.

"Whence comes this strange contrast? Why does the *élite* of the nation find itself in one of these halls more than in the other? Why does

[1] *The Federalist*, No. LXIII.

the first assembly unite so many vulgar elements,
while the second seems to have a monopoly of
talents and intelligence? Both emanate from
the people, and both are the product of universal
suffrage, and no voice, until now, has been raised
in the United States to say that the Senate was
the enemy of popular interests. Whence comes,
then, this enormous difference? I see only one
fact which explains it: the election which produces the House of Representatives is direct;
that which produces the Senate is submitted to
two degrees. The whole of the citizens elect the
legislature of each state, and the federal Constitution, transforming these legislatures in their
turn into electoral bodies, draws from them the
members of the Senate. The Senators, then,
express, although indirectly, the result of the
popular vote; for the legislature, which names
the Senators, is not an aristocratic or privileged
body, which derives its electoral rights from itself; it depends eventually on the whole of the
citizens. It is, in general, elected by them every
year, and they can always govern its decisions
by electing new members. But the popular will
has only to pass through this chosen assembly to
shape itself in some sort, and issue from it in a
nobler and finer form. The men thus elected
represent, then, always exactly the majority of
the nation which governs; but they represent

only the more elevated ideas which circulate among them, the generous instincts which animate them, and not the small passions which often agitate them and the vices which disgrace them. It is easy to foresee a time when the American Republic will be forced to multiply the two degrees in their electoral system, on pain of wrecking themselves miserably on the shores of democracy. I do not hesitate to avow it. I see in the double electoral degree the only means of bringing political liberty within the reach of all classes of the people." [1]

It is more than half a century since the electoral college, thus vaunted by its inventors, exerted any influence in the choice of the President. An attempt on the part of one of its members to use his own judgment in the matter would be treated as an act of the basest treachery. It has become a mere voting machine in the hands of the party. The office of " elector " has become an empty honor, accorded to such respectable members of the party as are unfit for, or do not desire, any more serious place. The candidates for the presidency are now chosen by a far larger body, which was never dreamed of by the makers of the Constitution, rarely bestows any thought on fitness as compared with popularity, and sits in the presence of an immense crowd which,

[1] *De la Démocratie en Amérique*, t. ii. p. 53.

though it does not actually take part in its proceedings, seeks to influence its decisions by every
species of noise and interruption.   In fact, all
show of deliberation has been abandoned by it.
Its action is settled beforehand by a small body
of men sitting in a private room.   The choice of
the delegates is prescribed, and may be finally
made under the influence of a secretly conducted
intrigue, of a " deal," or of a wild outburst of
enthusiasm known as a "stampede."   A greater
departure from the original idea of the electoral
college could hardly be imagined than the modern nominating convention.

Much the same phenomena are to be witnessed
in the case of the election of Senators by state
legislatures.   The machinery on which Tocqueville relied so confidently, the use of which he
expected to see spread, has completely broken
down.   The legislators have not continued to be
the kind of men he describes, and their choice
is not governed by the motives he looked for.
There is no longer such a thing as deliberation
by the legislatures, over the selection of the
Senators.   The candidate is selected by others,
who do not sit in the legislature at all, and they
supply the considerations which are to procure
him his election.   He is given the place either
on account of his past electioneering services to
the party, or on account of the largeness of his

contributions to its funds. The part he will play in the Senate rarely receives any attention. The anticipations of the framers of the Constitution, as set forth in the passage from "The Federalist" which I have quoted, have been in no way fulfilled. The members of the legislature, as a general rule, when acting as an electoral college, are very different from those whom the fathers of the republic looked for. In fact, the breakdown of their system is widespread, and appears to have exerted such a deteriorating influence on the character of the Senate, that we are witnessing the beginnings of an agitation for the election of Senators by the popular vote.

II

Why the founders and Tocqueville were mistaken about the double election as a check is easily explained. The founders knew little or nothing about democracy except what they got from Greek and Roman history; Tocqueville saw it at work only before the English traditions had lost their force. Democracy really means a profound belief in the wisdom as well as the power of the majority, not on certain occasions, but at whatever time it is consulted. All through American history this idea has had to struggle for assertion with the inherited political habits of the Anglo-Saxon race, which made

certain things " English " or " American " just as
to the Romans certain things were "Roman,"
for no reason that could be easily stated, except
that they were practices or beliefs of long standing. In England these habits have always composed what is called " the British Constitution,"
and in America they have made certain rights
seem immemorial or inalienable, such as the
right to a speedy trial by jury, the right to com-
pensation for property taken for public use, the
right to the decision of all matters in controversy by a court. This vague and ill-defined
creed existed before any constitution, and had
to be embodied in every constitution. The nearest approach to a name for it, in both countries,
is the " common law," or customs of the race, of
which, however, since it formed organized civilized societies, the courts of justice have always
been the fountains or exponents. We have had
to ask the judges in any given case what the
"common law " is, there being no written statement of it. It was consequently a comparatively
easy matter, in America, to get all questions in
any way affecting the life, liberty, or property
of individuals put into a fundamental law, to be
interpreted by the courts. Against this notion
of the fitness of things, democracy, or the wisdom of the majority, has beaten its head in
vain. That it should be hindered or delayed in

carrying out its will by a written instrument, expounded and applied by judges, has, therefore, always seemed natural.

In all the countries of Continental Europe, at the beginning of this century, it would have appeared a scandal or an anomaly that everybody should be liable to be called into court, no matter what office he held, on the plaint of a private man. With us the thing has always been a simple and inherent part of our system. But in the matter of appointment to office, which could have no effect upon or relation to private rights, pure democracy has never shown any disposition to be checked or gainsaid. It has never shown any inclination to treat public officers, from kings down, as other than its servants or the agents of its will. It revolted very early against Burke's definition of its representatives, as statesmen set to exercise their best judgment in watching over the people's interests. The democratic theory of the representative has always been that he is a delegate sent to vote, not for what he thinks best, but for what his constituents think best, even if it controverts his own opinion. The opposition to this view has been both feeble and inconstant ever since the early years of the century. The " delegate " theory has been gaining ground in England, and in America has almost completely succeeded in asserting its sway, so that we have seen many cases recently, in which members of Congress have openly declared their dissent from the measure for which they voted in obedience to their constituents.

It was this determination not to be checked in the selection of officers, but to make the people's will act directly on all nominations, which led to the early repudiation of the electoral college. That college was the device of those who doubted the wisdom and knowledge of the majority. But the majority was determined that in no matter within its jurisdiction should its wisdom and knowledge be questioned. It refused to admit that if it was competent to choose electors and members of Congress, it was not competent to choose the President. It accordingly set the electoral college ruthlessly aside at a very early period in the history of the republic. Tocqueville's idea that, in recognition of its own weakness and incompetence, it would spread the system of committing the appointing power to small select bodies of its own people, shows how far he was from comprehending the new force which had come into the world, and which he was endeavoring to analyze through observation of its working in American institutions.

It may seem at first sight as if this explanation does not apply to the failures of the legislatures to act upon their own judgment in the election of Senators. But the election of Senators has run exactly the same course as the nomination of Presidents; the choice has been taken out of the hands of the legislatures by the political party, and in each political party the people are represented by its managers, or "the machine," as it is called. They insist on nominating, or, if in a majority, on electing the Senators, just as they insist on nominating, or, if in a majority, on electing the President. Nearly every legislator is elected now with a view to the subsequent election of the Senators whenever there is a vacancy. His choice is settled for him beforehand. The casting of his vote is a mere formality, like the vote of the presidential electors. The man he selects for the place is the man already selected by the party. With this man's goodness or badness, fitness or unfitness, he does not consider that he has anything to do. Nothing can less resemble the legislature which filled the imagination of the framers of the Constitution than a legislature of our time assembled in joint convention to elect a Senator. It has hardly one of the characteristics which the writers of "The Federalist" ascribed to their ideal; it is little affected by any of the considerations which these gentlemen supposed would be predominant with it.

Any change, to be effective, must be a change in the mode of nomination. All attempts to limit or control the direct choice of the people, such as the use of the lot or of election by several degrees, as in Venice, must fail, and all machinery created for the purpose will probably pass away by evasion, if not by legislation. The difficulties of constitutional amendment are so great that it will be long before any legal change is made in the mode of electing Senators. It is not unsafe to assume that if any change be made in the mode of nomination, one of its first uses will be the practical imposition on all legislatures of the duty of electing to the Senate persons already designated by the voters at the polls.

As regards the state legislators themselves, it is well to remember that all political prophets require nearly as much time as the Lyell school of geologists. It is difficult enough to foresee what change will come about, but it is still more difficult to foretell how soon it will come about. No writer on politics should forget that it took five hundred years for Rome to fall, and fully a thousand years to educe modern Europe from the mediæval chaos. That the present legislative system of democracy will not last long there are abundant signs, but in what way it will be got rid of, or what will take its place, or how soon democratic communities will utterly tire of it, he would be a very rash speculator who would venture to say confidently. The most any one can do is to point out the tendencies which are likely to have most force, and to which the public seems to turn most hopefully.

At present, as far as one can see, the democratic world is filled with distrust and dislike of its parliaments, and submits to them only under the pressure of stern necessity. The alternative appears to be a dictatorship, but probably the world will not see another dictator chosen for centuries, if ever. Democracies do not admit that this is an alternative, nor do they admit that legislatures, such as we see them, are the last thing they have to try. They seem to be getting tired of the representative system. In no country is it receiving the praises it received forty years ago. There are signs of a strong disposition, which the Swiss have done much to stimulate, to try the "referendum" more frequently, on a larger scale, as a mode of enacting laws. One of the faults most commonly found in the legislatures, as I have already said, is the fault of doing too much. I do not think I exaggerate in saying that all the busier states in America, in which most capital is concentrated and most industry carried on, witness every meeting of the state legislature with anxiety and

alarm. I have never heard such a meeting
wished for or called for by a serious man outside
the political class. It creates undisguised fear
of some sort of interference with industry, some
sort of legislation for the benefit of one class, or
the trial of some hazardous experiment in judicial or administrative procedure, or in public
education or taxation. There is no legislature
to-day which is controlled by scientific methods,
or by the opinion of experts in jurisprudence or
political economy. Measures devised by such
men are apt to be passed with exceeding difficulty, while the law is rendered more and more
uncertain by the enormous number of acts passed
on all sorts of subjects.

Nearly every state has taken a step towards
meeting this danger by confining the meeting of
its legislature to every second year. It has said,
in other words, that it must have less legislation.
In no case that I have heard of has the opposition to this change come from any class except
the one that is engaged in the working of political machinery; that is, in the nomination or
election of candidates and the filling of places.
The rest of the community hails it with delight.
People are beginning to ask themselves why legislatures should meet even every second year; why
once in five years would not be enough. An
examination of any state statute-book discloses

the fact that necessary legislation is a rare thing; that the communities in our day seldom need a new law; and that most laws are passed without due consideration, and before the need of them has been made known, either by popular agitation, or by the demand of experts. It would not be an exaggeration to say that nine tenths of our modern state legislation will do no good, and that at least one tenth of it will do positive harm. If half the stories told about state legislatures be true, a very large proportion of the members meet, not with plans for the public good, but with plans either for the promotion of their personal interests, or for procuring money for party uses, or places for party agents.

The collection of such a body of men, not engaged in serious business, in the state capital, is not to be judged simply by the bills they introduce or pass. We have also to consider the opportunities for planning and scheming which the meetings offer to political jobbers and adventurers; and the effect, on such among them as still retain their political virtue, of daily contact with men who are there simply for illicit purposes, and with the swarm who live by lobbying, and get together every winter in order to trade in legislative votes. If I said, for instance, that the legislature at Albany was a school of vice, a fountain of political debauchery, and that few of the younger men came back from it without having learned to mock at political purity and public spirit, I should seem to be using unduly strong language, and yet I could fill nearly a volume with illustrations in support of my charges. The temptation to use their great power for the extortion of money from rich men and rich corporations, to which the legislatures in the richer and more prosperous Northern states are exposed, is great; and the legislatures are mainly composed of very poor men, with no reputation to maintain, or political future to look after. The result is that the country is filled with stories of scandals after every adjournment, and the press teems with abuse, which legislators have learned to treat with silent contempt or ridicule, so that there is no longer any restraint upon them. Their reëlection is not in the hands of the public, but in those of the party managers, who, as is shown in the Payn case in New York, find that they can completely disregard popular judgments on the character or history of candidates.

Side by side with the annual or biennial legislature, we have another kind of legislature, the "Constitutional Convention," which retains everybody's respect, and whose work, generally marked by care and forethought, compares creditably with the legislation of any similar body in the world.   Through the hundred years of national existence it has received little but favorable criticism from any quarter.   It is still an honor to have a seat in it.   The best men in the community are still eager or willing to serve in it, no matter at what cost to health or private affairs. I cannot recall one convention which has incurred either odium or contempt.   Time and social changes have often frustrated its expectations, or have shown its provisions for the public welfare to be inadequate or mistaken, but it is very rare indeed to hear its wisdom and integrity questioned.   In looking over the list of those who have figured in the conventions of the State of New York since the Revolution, one finds the name of nearly every man of weight and prominence ; and few lay it down without thinking how happy we should be if we could secure such service for our ordinary legislative bodies.

Now, what makes the difference ?   Three things, mainly.   First, the Constitutional Convention, as a rule, meets only once in about twenty years.   Men, therefore, who would not think of serving in an annual legislature, are ready on these rare occasions to sacrifice their personal convenience to the public interest.   Secondly, every one knows that the labors of the body, if adopted, will continue in operation without change for the best part of one's lifetime.

Thirdly, its conclusions will be subjected to the strictest scrutiny by the public, and will not be put in force without adoption by a popular vote. All this makes an American state constitution, as a rule, a work of the highest statesmanship, which reflects credit on the country, tends powerfully to promote the general happiness and prosperity, and is quoted or copied by foreign countries in the construction of organic laws.   The Constitutional Convention is as conspicuous an example of successful government as the state legislatures are of failure.   If we can learn anything from the history of these bodies, therefore, it is that if the meetings of the legislature were much rarer, say once in five or ten years, we should secure a higher order of talent and character for its membership and more careful deliberation for its measures, and should greatly reduce the number of the latter.   But we can go further, and say that inasmuch as all important matter devised by the convention is submitted to the people with eminent success, there is no reason why all grave measures of ordinary legislation should not be submitted also.   In other words, the referendum is not confined to Switzerland.[1]   We have it among us already.   All, or nearly all our state constitutions are the product of a referendum.   The number of important measures with

[1] Oberholtzer's *Referendum in America*, p. 15.

which the legislature feels chary about dealing,
which are brought before the people by its direction, increases every year.   Upon the question
of the location of the state capital and of some
state institutions, of the expenditure of public
money, of the establishment of banks, of the
maintenance or sale of canals, of leasing public
lands, of taxation beyond a certain amount, of
the prohibition of the liquor traffic, of the extension of the suffrage, and upon several other subjects, a popular vote is often taken in various
states.

In short, there is no discussion of the question
of legislatures in which either great restriction
in the number or length of their sessions, or the
remission of a greatly increased number of subjects to treatment by the popular vote, does not
appear as a favorite remedy for their abuses and
shortcomings.   If we may judge by these signs,
the representative system, after a century of
existence, under a very extended suffrage, has
failed to satisfy the expectations of its earlier
promoters, and is likely to make way in its turn
for the more direct action of the people on the
most important questions of government, and a
much-diminished demand for all legislation whatever.   This, at all events, is the only remedy
now in sight, which is much talked about or is
considered worthy of serious attention.

PECULIARITIES OF AMERICAN MUNICI-
PAL GOVERNMENT

In trying to deduce from American examples some idea of the probable influence of modern democracy on city government, we have to bear in mind that the municipal history of America differs greatly from that of Europe. In Europe, as a general rule, municipalities either existed before the state, or grew up in spite of the state; that is, they were fresh attempts to keep alive the sparks of civilization in the Middle Ages, before anything worthy of the name of a state had been organized, or else they sprang into being as a refuge from or a protest against state despotism. In either case they always had a life of their own, and often a very vigorous and active life. No European city can be said to have owed its growth to the care or authority of the central power. Both kings and nobles looked on cities with suspicion and jealousy; charters were granted, in the main, with reluctance, and often had to be retained or extorted, by force of arms. These classes recognized liberties or franchises which already existed, rather than granted new privileges or powers. Municipal life was either an inheritance from the Roman Empire, or an attempt at social reorganization in a period of general anarchy.

American cities, on the contrary, are without exception the creations of a state; they have grown up either under state supervision or through state instigation; that is, they owe their origin and constitution to the government. Their charters have usually been devised or influenced by people who did not expect to live in them, and who had no personal knowledge of their special needs. In other words, an American municipal charter has been rather the embodiment of an *à priori* view of the kind of thing a city ought to be, than a legal recognition of preëxisting wants and customs. The complete predominance of the state has been a leading idea in the construction of all American charters. No legislature has been willing to encourage the growth of an independent municipal life. No charter has been looked on as a finality or as organic law. In fact, the modification or alteration of charters has been a favorite occupation of legislatures, stimulated by the rapid growth of the cities and by the absence of all historical experience of municipal life.

The idea most prominent in American municipal history is that cities are simply places in which population is more than usually concentrated. Down to the outbreak of the war this view worked fairly well in most cases. The cities were small, their wants were few, and the inhabitants had little or no thought of any organization differing much from ordinary town government. Gas, water, police, and street-cleaning had not become distinct municipal needs. Pigs were loose in the streets of New York until 1830, and Boston had no mayor until 1822. Generally, too, the government was administered by local notables. Immigration had not begun to make itself seriously felt until 1846, and down to 1830, at least, it was held an honor to be a New York alderman. For the work of governing cities or making charters for them, the average country legislator was considered abundantly competent. It presented none of what we now call " problems." The result was that new or altered charters were very frequent. The treatment of the city as a separate entity, with wants and wishes of its own and entitled to a voice in the management of its own affairs, was something unknown or unfamiliar. In 1857, when, under the influence of the rising tide of immigration, the affairs of New York as a municipality seemed to become unmanageable, the only remedy thought of was the appointment of state commissioners to take into their own hands portions of the city business, such as the police, the construction of a park, and so on.

The crisis in the affairs of the city of New York which is known as the Tweed period was simply the complete breakdown of this old plan of managing the affairs of the city through the legislature. Tweed could hardly have succeeded in his schemes if he had not had the state legislature at his back, and had not been able to procure such changes in the charter as were necessary for his purpose. He pushed his régime to its legitimate consequences. In fact, his career is entitled to the credit of having first made city government a question, or " problem," of American politics. I doubt much whether, previous to his day, any American had considered it as being, or likely to become, a special difficulty of universal suffrage. But his successful rise and troublesome career now presented to the public, in a new and startling light, the impossibility of governing cities effectively by treating them as merely pieces of thickly peopled territory. Ever since his time the municipal difficulty has been before men's minds as something to be dealt with somehow; but for a long time no one knew exactly how to deal with it.

There was an American way, already well known, of meeting other difficulties of government, but the American way of governing large cities under a pure democracy, no one seemed to have considered. The American way of curing all evils had hitherto been simply to turn out the party in power, and try the other. It had always been assumed that the party in power would dread overthrow sufficiently to make it " behave well;" or, if it did not, that its overthrow would act as a warning which would prevent its successor's repeating its errors. This system had always been applied successfully to federal and state affairs; why should it not be applied to city affairs? Accordingly it was so applied to city affairs, without a thought of any other system, down to 1870. But in 1870 it began to dawn on people that party government of great cities would hardly do any longer. City government, it was seen, is in some sense a business enterprise, and must be carried out either by the kind of men one would make directors of a bank or trustees of an estate, or else by highly trained officials.

The first of these methods is not open any longer in America. One can hardly say that the respect for notables no longer exists in American cities, but it does not exist as a political force or expedient. The habit of considering conspicuous inhabitants as entitled to leading municipal places must be regarded as lost.

In a large city conspicuousness is rare, and widespread knowledge of a man's character or fitness for any particular office is difficult. Moreover, among the class which has already made proof of ability in other callings, readiness to undertake onerous public duties is not often to be met with. Consequently, with few exceptions, the government of successful modern cities has to be intrusted to experts, and to get experts salaries must be large, and tenure permanent. A competent professional man cannot, as a rule, be induced to accept a poorly paid place for a short term. Almost as soon as public attention began to be turned to the subject, the practice began of seeking these experts through party organizations. But the most important offices in cities are elective, and the idea that any elective office could be divorced from party, or could be made non-partisan, was wholly unfamiliar to the American mind. Ever since the Union was established, men had always filled offices, if they could, with persons who agreed with them, and with whom they were in the habit of acting in federal affairs. That city offices could be an exception to this rule was an idea which, when first produced twenty-five years ago, was deemed ridiculous, and is even yet not thoroughly established among the mass of the voters. The belief that offices were "spoils" or perquisites was, unfortunately, most dominant during the years of great immigration which preceded and immediately followed the war, and became imbedded in the minds of the newcomers as peculiarly "American." With this came, not unnaturally, the notion that no one would serve faithfully, in any official place, the party to which he did not belong. Full party responsibility, it was said, required that every place under the government, down to the lowest clerkship, should be filled by members of the party in power.

In no place did this notion find readier acceptance than in cities, because the offices in them were so numerous, and the elections so frequent, and the salaries, as compared with those of the country, so high. The possession of the city government, too, meant the possibility of granting a large number of illicit favors. For the laborer, there was sure employment and easy work in the various public departments; for the public-house keeper, there was protection against the execution of the liquor laws by the police; for the criminal classes, there was slack prosecution by the district attorney, or easy "jury fixing" by the commissioner of jurors; for the contractor, there were profitable jobs and much indulgence for imperfect execution; for the police, there were easy discipline and impunity for corrupt abuses of power. In fact, the cities furnished a perfect field for the practice of the spoils system, and the growth in them of rings and organizations like Tammany was the natural and inevitable consequence. No such organization could be created for charitable purposes, or for the mere diffusion of religious or political opinions. It was made possible in New York by the number of places and benefits at its disposal. The effect on the imagination of the newly arrived emigrant, whether Irish or German, was very great. It shut out from his view both city and state as objects of his allegiance, and made recognition by the "leader" of the district in which he lived the first object of his ambition in his new country.

What is true of New York is true, *mutatis mutandis*, of all the other large cities, — Philadelphia, Chicago, Cincinnati, St. Louis. They all have an organization resembling Tammany, created and maintained by the same means; and at the head of the organization there is a man, ignorant perhaps of all other things, but gifted with unusual capacity for controlling the poor and dependent, who has come since Tweed's day to be known as a "boss." He arises naturally as a condition of success, and if he has favors to bestow he arises all the more rapidly. The boss is, in short, the inevitable product of the spoils system. He must have sensible advantages to give away in order to retain his power, and he is necessary for their effective distribution. There has to be some one to say decisively who is to have this or that office or prize, who deserves it, and whose services cannot be had without it. There could hardly be a better proof and illustration of this than the way in which the boss system has spread all over the country. In all cities and in many states every political organization now has a similar officer at its head. It remained for some time after Tweed's day the reproach of the Democrats that they submitted to an arbitrary ruler of this kind, but the Republicans are nearly everywhere imitating them. There are but few states, and there is no large city, in which the offices or nominations for office are not parceled out by one man acting in the name of an "organization." Tweed's control of the city and legislature was not more complete than is Platt's in New York or Quay's in Pennsylvania. The system is evidently one which saves trouble, and makes it easier to secure the blind obedience of large masses of men. Its end is bad, but that it attains this end there can be no doubt.

It can thus be easily seen that no American city has ever been administered with reference to its own interests. In not one, until our own time, has there been even a pretense of non-par-

tisanship; that is, the filling of the offices solely
with a view to efficiency in the discharge of their
duties. As a rule, they have been filled with a
view to the promotion of opinions on some federal question, such as the tariff, or as a reward
for services rendered at federal elections. The
state of things thus produced in American cities
closely resembles the state of things produced in
the Middle Ages by religious intolerance, when
the main concern of governments was not so
much to promote the material interests of their
subjects, as to maintain right opinions with regard to the future life. The filling of a city
office by a man simply because he holds certain
views regarding the tariff, or the currency, or
the banks, is very like appointing him to an
office of state because he is a good Catholic or
can conscientiously sign the Thirty-Nine Arti-
cles; that is to say, his fitness for his real duties
is not a consideration of importance in filling
the place. No private business could be carried
on in this way, and it is doubtful whether any
attempt to carry it on in this way was ever made.
But the temptation to resort to it under party
government and universal suffrage is strong, for
the reasons which I have tried to set forth in
treating of the nominating system. The task of
inducing large bodies of men to vote in a particular way is such, that it is hardly wonderful

that party managers should use every means within their reach for its performance.

One of the effects of the system, and possibly the worst and most difficult to deal with, is the veiling of the city from the popular eye, as the main object of allegiance and attention, by what is called " the organization," namely, the club or society, presided over by the boss, which manages party affairs. The tendency among men who take a strong interest in politics to look upon the organization as their real master, to boast of their devotion to it as a political virtue, to call themselves " organization men," and to consider the interests of the organization as paramount to those of the city at large, is an interesting development of party government. All political parties originate in a belief that a certain idea can be best spread, or a certain policy best promoted, by the formation of an organization for the purpose. The other belief, that one's own party is fittest for power, and deserves support even when it makes mistakes, easily follows. This is very nearly the condition of the public mind about federal parties. A large number of votes are cast at every federal election merely to show confidence in the party, rather than approval of its position with regard to any specific question. There is a still further stage in the growth of party spirit, in which the voter supports his party, right or wrong, no matter how much he may condemn its policy or its acts, on the ground that it is made up of better material than the other party, and that the latter, if in power, would be more dangerous. The Republican party, in particular, commands a great deal of support, especially from the professional and educated classes throughout the country, on these grounds. They vote for it as the least wrong or least likely to be mischievous, even if they feel unable to vote for it as wise or pure.

But in the cities still another advance has been made, and the parties have really been separated from politics altogether, and treated, without disguise, as competitors for the disposal of a certain number of offices and the handling of a certain amount of money. The boss on either side rarely pretends to have any definite opinions on any federal question, or to concern himself about them. He proclaims openly that his side has the best title to the offices, and the reason he gives for this is, generally, that the other side has made what he considers mistakes. He hardly ever pleads merits of his own. In fact, few or none of the bosses have ever been writers or speakers, or have ever been called on to discuss public questions or have opinions about them. The principal ones, Tweed, Kelly, Croker, Platt, and Quay, have been either silent or illiterate men, famed for their reticence, and have plumed themselves on their ability to *do* things without talk. In New York, they have succeeded in diffusing among the masses, to a certain extent, the idea that a statesman should not talk, but simply " fix things," and vote the right way; that is, they have divorced discussion from politics. One of the boss's amusements, when he is disposed to be humorous, is doing something or saying something to show how little influence voters and writers have on affairs. In the late senatorial canvass in New York, a number of letters commending one of the candidates, who happened to be the Republican boss, were published, most of them from young men, and it was interesting to see how many commended silence as one of the best attributes of a Senator.

Consequently, nearly all discussions of city affairs are discussions about places. What place a particular man will get, what place he is trying to get, and by what disappointment about places he is chagrined, or " disgruntled," as the term is, form the staple topics of municipal debates. The rising against Tammany in 1894, which resulted in the election of Mayor Strong, to some extent failed to produce its due effect, owing to his refusal to distribute places so as to satisfy Mr. Platt, the Republican leader; or, in other words, to give Mr. Platt the influence in distributing the patronage to which he held that he was entitled. This led to the frustration, or long delay, of the legislation which was necessary to make the overthrow of Tammany of much effect. Some of the necessary bills the legislature, which was controlled by Platt, refused to pass, and others it was induced to pass only by great effort and after long postponement. No reason was ever assigned for this hostility to Strong's proposals, except failure in the proper distribution of offices. No doubt a certain amount of discussion of plans for city improvement has gone on, but it has gone on among a class which has no connection with politics and possesses little political influence. The class of politicians, properly so called, commonly refuses to interest itself in any such discussions, unless it can be assured beforehand that the proposed improvements will be carried out by certain persons of their own selection, who are seldom fit for the work.

In addition to reliance on change of parties for the improvement of city government, much dependence has been placed on the old American theory that when things get very bad, sufficient popular indignation will be roused to put an end to them; that the evil will be eradicated by something in the nature of a revolution, as in

the case of Tweed and of the Tammany abuses
in 1894. But this theory, as regards cities, has
to be received with much modification. Popular indignation is excited by violent departures
from popular standards ; the popular conscience
has to be shocked by striking disregard of the
tests established by popular usage; in order that
this may happen, the popular conscience has to
be kept, if I may use the expression, in a state
of training. Now, for the mass of such voters
as congregate in great cities, training for the
public conscience consists largely in the spectacle of good government. Their standards depend largely on what they see. People must
have a certain familiarity with something better,
— that is, must either remember or see it, — in
order to be really discontented with their present lot. But when once the mass of men have
obtained liberty and security, it becomes increasingly difficult to rouse them into activity about
matters of apparently less consequence. In
other words, incompetence or corruption in the
work of administration being rarely visible to
the public eye, the masses are not as easily
shocked by it as they are by bad legislation, or
by such interferences with personal liberty as
liquor or other sumptuary laws. Their notion
of what ought to be, is largely shaped by what
is. The political education of the people in a

democracy, especially in large cities, is to a considerable degree the work of the government. The way in which they see things done becomes in their eyes the way in which they ought to be done ; the kind of men they see in public office becomes the kind of men they think fit for public office. The part the actual government plays in forming the political ideals of the young is one of the neglected but most important topics of political discussion. Our youth learn far more of the real working of our institutions by observation of the men elected or appointed to office, particularly to the judicial and legislative offices, than from school-books or newspapers. The election of a notoriously worthless or corrupt man as a judge or member of the legislature makes more impression on a young mind than any chapter in a governmental manual, or any college lecture.

For this reason, the application of the civil service rules to subordinate city offices, which has now been in existence in New York and Boston for many years, is an extremely important contribution to the work of reform, however slow its operation may be. To make known to the public that to get city places a man must come up to the standard of fitness ascertained by competitive examination is not simply a means of improving the municipal service, but an educative process of a high order. The same thing may be said of such matters as the expulsion from office of the Tammany police justices by the general removal act, passed when Mr. Strong came into office in 1895, in spite of all the blemishes in its execution. It made clear to the popular mind, as nothing else could, that a certain degree of character and education was necessary to the discharge of even minor judicial functions, and that the Tammany standard of " common sense " and familiar acquaintance with the criminal classes was not sufficient. The covert or open opposition to what is called civil service reform, on the part of nearly the whole political class in cities, goes to confirm this view. There could be no greater blow to the existing system of political management than the withdrawal of the offices from arbitrary disposal by the bosses. The offices have been for half a century the chief or only means of rewarding subordinate agents for political work and activity.

One effect, and a marked one, of this withdrawal has been the introduction of the practice of levying blackmail on corporations, nominally for political purposes. Nothing is known certainly about the amounts levied in this way, but there are two thousand corporations in New York exposed to legislative attack, and in the aggregate their contributions must reach a very large sum. Since the boss has obtained command of the legislature as well as of the city, — that is, since Tweed's time, — they are literally at the mercy of the legislature, or, in other words, at *his* mercy. Their taxes may be raised, or, in the case of gas companies or railroad companies, their charges lowered. The favorite mode of bringing insurance companies to terms is ordering an examination of their assets, which may be done through the superintendent of insurance, who is an appointee of the governor and Senate, or, virtually, of the boss. This examination has to be paid for by the company, and, I am told, may be made to cost $200,000 ; it is usually conducted by politicians out of a job, of a very inferior class. To protect themselves from annoyances of this sort, the corporations, which it must be remembered are creations of the law, and increase in number every year, are only too glad to meet the demands of the boss. Any " campaign " contribution, no matter how large, and it is sometimes as high as $50,000 or even $100,000, is small compared to the expense which he can inflict on them by his mere fiat. Of course this is corruption, and the corporations know it. The officers, however high they may stand in point of business character, submit to it, or connive at it. In many cases, if not in most, they even confess it. They defend their compliance, too, on grounds which carry one back a long way in the history of settled government. That is, they say that their first duty is to protect the enormous amount of property committed to their charge, a large portion of which belongs to widows and orphans ; that if they have any duty at all in the matter of reforming municipal and state administration, it is a secondary and subordinate one, which should not be performed at the cost of any damage to these wards ; that, therefore, the sum they pay to the boss may be properly considered as given to avert injury against which the law affords no protection. They maintain that in all this matter they are victims, not offenders, and that the real culprit is the government of the State, which fails to afford security to property in the hands of a certain class of owners.

I will not attempt to discuss here the soundness of this view in point of morality. It is to be said, in extenuation at least, that the practices of which the corporations are accused prevail all over the Union, in city and in country, East and West. I have had more than one admission made to me by officers of companies that they kept an agent at the state capital during sessions of the legislature for the express purpose of shielding them, by means of money, against legislative attacks, and that without this they could not carry on business. It has been the custom, I am afraid, to a greater or less extent, for corporations to keep such agents at the state capitals ever since corporations became at all numerous and rich, — for fully fifty years. What is peculiar and novel about the present situation is that the boss has become a general agent for all the companies, and saves them the trouble of keeping one at their own cost, in Albany or Harrisburg, or in any other state capital. He receives what they wish or are expected to pay, and in return he guarantees them the necessary protection. He is thus the channel through which pass all payments made by any one for " campaign " purposes. If his party is not in office he receives very little, barely enough to assure him of good will. When his party is in power, as the power is his, there need be practically no limit to his demands.

If it be asked why the corporations do not themselves revolt against this system and stop it by exposure, the answer is simple enough. In the first place, most of the corporations have rivals, and dread being placed at a disadvantage by some sort of persecution from which competitors may have bought exemption. The thing which they dread most is business failure or defeat. For this they are sure to be held accountable by stockholders or by the public;

for submitting to extortion, they may not be held accountable by anybody. In the next place, the supervision exercised by the state officers being lax or corrupt, the corporations are likely to be law-breakers in some of their practices, and to dread exposure or inquiry. In many cases, therefore, they are doubtless only too glad to buy peace or impunity, and this their oppressors probably know very well. Last of all, and perhaps the most powerful among the motives for submission, is the fear of vengeance in case they should not succeed. A corporation which undertook to set the boss at defiance, would enter on a most serious contest, with little chance of success. All the influences at his command, political and judicial, would be brought into play for its defeat. Witnesses would disappear, or refuse to answer. Juries would be "fixed;" judges would be technical and timid; the press would be bought up by money or advertising, or by political influence; other motives than mere resistance to oppression would be invented and imputed; the private character of the officers would be assailed. In short, the corporation would probably fail, or appear to fail, in proving its case, and would find itself substantially foiled in its undertaking, after having expended a great deal of money, and having excited the bitter enmity of the boss and of all the active politicians among his followers. It can hardly be expected that a company would make such an attempt without far stronger support than it would receive from the public, owing to the general belief that no corporation would come into court with clean hands. How little effect public support would give in such a contest, as long as the power of the boss over the legislators and state officials continues, through the present system of nomination, may be inferred from what has happened in the case of the enlargement of the city of New York, known as the Greater New York Bill.[1]

[1] The history of this measure has been so concisely written by Mr. J. B. Bishop that I cannot avoid quoting him : —

"The most impressive demonstration of the despotic power behind these decisions was made in connection with the proposed charter for Greater New York. This had been drawn by the commission created by the act of 1896. It had been prepared in secret, and only very inadequate opportunity had been given for public inspection of it before it was sent to the legislature ; yet, in the brief time afforded, it had been condemned in very strong terms by what I may truthfully call the organized and individual intelligence of the community. The Bar Association, through a committee which contained several of the leading lawyers of the city, subjected it to expert legal examination, and declared it to be so full of defects and confusing provisions as to be 'deplorable,' and to give rise, if made law, 'to mischiefs far outweighing any benefits which might reasonably be expected to flow from it.' The Chamber of Commerce, the Board of Trade, the Clearing House Association, the City Club, the Union League Club, the Reform Club, the Real Estate Exchange, all the reputable ex-mayors and other officials, expressed equally strong condemnation, especially of certain leading provisions of the instrument ; and the legislature was formally re-

The subjection of the city to the person who controls the legislature is secured in part by the use of federal and possibly city offices, and in part by the extortion of money from property-

quested to give more time to the subject by postponing the date on which the charter should become operative. Not the slightest attention was paid at Albany to any of these requests. The Bar Association's objections were passed over in silence, as indeed were all the protests. The charter, excepting a few trifling changes, was passed without amendment by both Houses of the legislature by an overwhelming vote. Only six of the one hundred and fourteen Republican members voted against it in the Assembly, and only one of the thirty-six Republican members in the Senate. There was no debate upon it in the Assembly. The men who voted for the charter said not a word in its favor, and not a word in explanation of their course in voting against all proposals to amend it. In the Senate, the charter's chief advocates declared frankly their belief that it was a measure of ' political suicide,' since it was certain to put the proposed enlarged city into the hands of their opponents, the Democrats ; yet they all voted for it because it had been made a party measure, — that is, the despot had said it must pass. After its first passage, it was sent, for public hearings and approval, to the mayors of the three cities affected by its provisions. The opposition developed at the hearings in New York city was very impressive, — so much so that Mayor Strong, who, as an *ex officio* member of the charter commission, had signed the report which had accompanied it when it went to the legislature, was moved by a ' strong sense of public duty ' to veto it because of ' serious and fundamental defects.' When the charter, with his veto message, arrived in Albany, the two Houses passed it again by virtually the same vote as at first, and without either reading the mayor's message, or more than barely mentioning his name. One of the members who voted for it said privately, ' If it were not for the fact that the " old man " wants it, I doubt if the charter would get a dozen votes in the legislature outside the Brooklyn and Long Island members.' "

holders, for purposes of corruption; and all remedy for this is impeded or wholly hindered by the interest of city voters in matters other than municipal.

The earliest remedy, — the substitution of one party in the city government for another, — which has been employed steadily by each party for the last half century with singular acquiescence on the part of the public, has been to some degree supplanted, since the war, by another, namely, the modification of the charter, so as to secure greater concentration of power in few hands. More and more authority has been withdrawn from the bodies elected for purposes of legislation, and has been transferred to the bodies elected for purposes of administration. Before the late change in the city charter, the New York board of aldermen, by a process of deprivation pursued through long years, was bereft of all but the most insignificant powers. The preparation of the city estimates and the imposition of the city taxes, two peculiarly legislative duties, were transferred bodily to a small board composed of the mayor and heads of departments. Nearly every change in charters has armed the mayor with more jurisdiction. This movement has run on lines visible in almost all democratic communities. The rise of the boss is distinctly one of its results. There is everywhere a tendency to remit to a single person the supreme direction of large bodies of men animated with a common purpose or bound together by common ideas.   One sees in this person dim outlines of the democratic Cæsar of the Napoleonic era, but he differs in that he has to do his work under the full glare of publicity, has to be able to endure " exposure " and denunciation by a thousand newspapers, and to bear overthrow by combinations among his own followers with equanimity, and has to rely implicitly on " management " rather than on force.

The difficulty of extracting from a large democracy an expression of its real will is, in fact, slowly becoming manifest.   It is due partly to the size of the body, and partly to the large number of voters it must necessarily contain who find it troublesome to make up their minds, or who fail to grasp current questions, or who love and seek guidance in important transactions.   On most of the great national questions of our day, except in exciting times, a large proportion of the voters do not hold their opinions with much firmness or tenacity, or with much distinctness. On one point in particular, which has great importance in all modern democracies, — the effect of any specific measure on the party prospects, — the number of men who have clear ideas is very small.   The mass to be influenced is so large, and the susceptibilities of different localities differ so widely, that fewer and fewer persons, except those who "have their hand on the machine," venture on a confident prediction as to the result of an election. The consequence is that those who do hold clean-cut opinions, and pronounce them with courage, speedily acquire influence and authority, almost in spite of themselves. Indeed, almost every influence now in operation, both in politics and in business, tends to the concentration of power. The disposition to combine several small concerns into one large one, to consolidate corporations, and to convert private partnerships into companies, is but an expression of the general desire to remit the work of management or administration to one man or to a very few men. In all considerable bodies who wish to act together for common objects, the many are anxious to escape the responsibility of direction, and, naturally enough, this has shown itself in city government as well as in party government.

This tendency has been temporarily obscured in New York by the consolidation of the suburbs into what is called the Greater New York. In order to secure this, that is, to obtain the consent of "the politicians," it has been found necessary to revive the old, long-tried, and much-condemned plan of a city legislature with two branches, a

number of boards, and a wide diffusion of responsibility.   There is about this new machinery
an appearance of local representative self-government, but it is only an appearance.   The real
power of interference, change, or modification
still resides in the legislature at Albany, and the
habit of interference is already formed and
active.

What modern municipalities need, especially
in America, is a régime in which, without hesitation, without study, without lawyers' or experts' opinions, the humblest laborer can tell who
is responsible for any defect he may discover
in the police of the streets, in the education of
his children, or in the use and mode of his taxation.

To secure such a régime, however, the control
of state legislatures in America over cities must
be either reduced or destroyed, and this seems
the task which, above all, has first to be accomplished by municipal reforms; it is really
the one in which they are now engaged, though,
apparently, sometimes unconsciously. The "hearings" of leading citizens by legislative committees, which almost invariably accompany the
passage by state legislatures of measures affecting municipal government, are in the nature of
protests against legislative action, or assertions
of the incompetency of the legislature to deal

with the matter in hand. The contemptuous indifference with which they are generally treated is simply an assertion that, under no circumstances, will the legislature surrender its power. This has been curiously illustrated by the recent complete refusal of the New York legislature to pay any attention to the power of veto given to the mayors of New York cities by the late constitutional convention. This provision has had so little effect that a mayor's objections to any particular piece of legislation are not even discussed, much less answered. It has seemed as if the legislature were unwilling to allow it to be supposed that it could ever be in any way influenced by the criticism or suggestion of local notables. All American legislatures have long shown unwillingness to adopt suggestions or submit to interference from the outside. Few, if any, of the numerous reports of commissions on taxation or municipal government or other subjects made during the last thirty years, have received any attention.

There is another reason why state legislatures are unwilling to relinquish their control of cities, and it is nearly as potent as any; that is, the accumulation of wealth in the cities as compared to the country. One of the peculiarities of an agricultural population is the small amount of cash it handles. Farmers, as a general rule, live

to some extent on their own produce, wear old
clothes, as people are apt to do in the country,
pay no house-rent, very rarely divert themselves
by " shopping," and seldom see any large sum
of money except at their annual sales after har-
vest. In short, as compared with an urban population, they live with what seems great economy.
The temptations to small expenses which so constantly beset a city man seldom come in their way.
Their standard of living in dress, food, clothing,
and furniture is much lower than that of a city
population of a corresponding class. The result
is that money has a much greater value in their
eyes than in those of the commercial class.
They part with a dollar more reluctantly; they
think it ought to go farther. They look on a
city man's notion of salaries as utterly extravagant or unreasonable, and to receive such salaries
seems to them almost immoral. City life they
consider marked throughout by gross extravagance.

Moreover, the farmer finds it very difficult to
place a high value on labor which is not done
with the hands and does not involve exposure to
weather. Difference of degree in value of such
labor it is hard, if not impossible, to estimate.
The expense of training for an intellectual occupation, such as a lawyer's or a doctor's, he is not
willing to take into account. One consequence

of this has been that, though almost all servants of the government — judges, secretaries, collectors — live in cities or by city standards, their salaries are fixed not so much by the market value of their services, as by the farmer's notion of what is reasonable; for the farmer is as yet the ruling power in America. The salaries of the federal judges, for instance, were fixed at the establishment of the government by the largest annual earnings of a lawyer of the highest standing of that day; they are now about one fourth of what such a lawyer earns, and it would be difficult or impossible to increase them. The farmer's inability, too, to estimate degrees in the value of such services leads him to suppose that what they are worth is the sum for which anybody will undertake to render them, and that if any member of the bar offered to discharge the duties of a judge of the Supreme Court for one thousand dollars a year, it would be proper enough to accept his services at that rate. This great difference has some important political consequences also. It leads to agricultural distrust of urban views on finance, and produces in country districts a deep impression of city recklessness and greed. City exchanges, whether stock or produce, are supposed by the farmer to be the resorts of gamblers rather than instruments of legitimate business.

In truth, the difference in needs and interests and points of view between the city and the country arises almost as soon as anything which can be called a city comes into existence. Close contact with many other men, familiarity with the business of exchanging commodities, the necessity for frequent coöperation, all help to convert the inhabitant of cities into a new type of man. The city man has always been a polished or " urbane " man. The distinction between him and the " rustic," in mind and manners, has in all ages been among the commonplaces of literature. One material effect of this difference is that the urban man has been an object of slight dislike or jealousy to the country man. His greater alertness of mind, which comes from much social intercourse, and familiarity with trade and commerce, makes him in some degree an object of suspicion to the latter, who constantly dreads being outwitted by him. Cities, too, have always been to the country man resorts of vice of one sort or another, and all that he hears of the temptations of city life fills him with a sense of his own moral superiority. To the poet and to the farmer the country has been the seat of virtue, simplicity, and purity ; the one moralist who practiced his own precepts was the rustic moralist. It has been very natural, therefore, that in America, in which the country has had the power before the city, and not, as in Europe, the city before the country, the country should have tried with peculiar care to retain its free domination over the city.

This process has been made easy, not only by the fact that the city was generally created by the state, but by our practice of selecting our state capitals, not for judicial, or commercial, or historical, but for topographical considerations. No other people has been in the habit, or has had the opportunity, of choosing places for its political capitals at all. In all other countries, if I am not mistaken, the capitals were made by trade, or commerce, or manufactures, or some ancient drift of population. But in many of our states the political capital is not the chief city in wealth or population; it owes its political preëminence to the fact that it was within easy reach from all parts of the state, in the days when travel was slow and difficult, — a circumstance now of no importance whatever. Were capitals selected with us by the agencies to which they owe their existence in the Old World, New York would be the capital of the State of New York, Philadelphia of Pennsylvania, Cincinnati of Ohio, Chicago of Illinois, and Detroit of Michigan.

The present arrangement has proved unfor-

tunate in two ways : it has helped to confirm
the rural mind in a belief in the inferiority and
insignificance of cities as compared to the country ; and it has kept legislators, when in session,
secluded from the observation of the most ac-
tive-minded portion of the population, and from
intercourse with them, and has deprived them of
the information and the new ideas which such
intercourse brings with it. Members of Congress and of the state legislatures suffer seriously in mind and character from our practice
of cutting them off, during their official lives,
from communion with the portion of the population most immersed in affairs, and of keeping
them out of sight of those who are most competent to understand their action and to criticise
it. No one who has paid much attention to our
political life can have helped observing the injurious effect on the legislative mind of massing
legislators together in remote towns, in which
they exchange ideas only with one another, and
get no inkling of the real drift of public opinion
about a particular measure until it has been irre-
vocably acted upon. There is no question that
this has been in all parts of the country a powerful aid to the boss in preserving his domination.
Nothing can suit his purpose better than to get
his nominees together in some remote corner of
the state, in which he can instruct them in their

duties and watch their action without disturbance from outside currents of criticism or suggestion. Every legislature is the better, and its tone is the healthier, for being kept in close contact with the leading centres of business in the community, and hearing daily or hourly from its men of affairs. Much of the ignorance about exchange, credit, and currency, and of the suspicion of bankers and men of business, which has shown itself in our legislative capitals in late years, has been due to the isolation of the rural legislator from social intercourse with men engaged in other pursuits than his own.

But the most serious drawback in the practice of making political capitals to order is undoubtedly its tendency to lessen the rural legislator's sense of the importance of cities, and to increase his readiness to interfere in their government without any real knowledge of their needs. This readiness is one of the greatest difficulties of American municipal government. It arises, as I have said, partly from the historical antecedents of our cities; partly from the countryman's sense of moral superiority, in which the clergy and the poets try to confirm him; and partly from the fear inspired by the rapid growth of the cities in population, and the belief that their interests are in some manner different from those of the country. This belief found expression in the provision of the New York Constitution that the new city and county of New York should never be represented by more than half the state Senate. There is a vague fear diffused through the rural districts that if the cities should get the upper hand in the state government, or should succeed in achieving even a quasi-independence, some serious consequence to the whole community would follow. But to have any fear on the subject is to question the whole democratic theory. The system of political division into states and districts and counties, with separate representation, is an admission that different localities have different interests, of which other localities are not competent to take charge. It is on this idea that local self-government is based. It is the principal reason why New York does not govern Massachusetts, or Buffalo govern New York.

In the case of cities this difference is simply magnified, and the incompetency of other districts or counties for the work of their management is made more than usually plain. To suppose that a city is less fit to govern itself than are more thinly peopled districts, or that its political ascendency would contain danger to the state, is to abandon the democratic theory. In a democratic community there is really no conflict of interests between city and country ; the prosperity of one makes the prosperity of the other. Neither can grow rich by the impoverishment of the other. From the democratic point of view, a city is merely a very large collection of people in one spot, with many wants peculiar to such large collections. To deny its fitness to govern itself is to deny the majority principle with strong emphasis. Nevertheless, the attempts hitherto made in America to secure reform in the administration of cities have been almost exclusively efforts to wrest greater powers of local administration from the state legislatures, which consist in the main of farmers, who have no special interest in cities whatever, but who are indomitable champions of local self-government in all other political divisions. In three states only, as yet, Missouri, California, and Washington, have the cities succeeded in securing a constitutional right to approve their own charters before they go into operation, which is the furthest step in advance that has been made. In twenty-three states they are constitutionally secured against having special charters made for them by the legislature, with or without their consent. Whatever sort of organic law is imposed in one city in these states must be imposed in all. But in ten states the cities are still at the mercy of the legislature, which may govern them by special legislation,

and make, amend, or annul charters at its discretion, without pity or remorse.

In looking at the history and condition of
municipalities in America, one consideration
meets us at every stage; that is, that in no other
civilized country is municipal government so
completely within the control of public opinion.
Everywhere else there are deeply rooted traditions, long-established customs, much-respected
vested rights and cherished prejudices, to be
dealt with, before any satisfactory framework of
city government can be set up.   Here the whole
problem is absolutely at the disposal of popular
sentiment.   Our cities, therefore, might most
easily have been the model cities of the modern
world.   Birmingham and Glasgow and Berlin,
in other words, ought to have been in America.
It is we who ought to have shown the Old
World how to live comfortably in great masses
in one place.   We have no city walls to pull
down, or ghettos to clear out, or guilds to buy
up, or privileges to extinguish.   We have simply to provide health, comfort, and education, in
our own way, according to the latest experience
in science, for large bodies of free men in one
spot.

This is as much as saying that in talking of
the municipal question we describe a state of the
popular mind, and not a state of law.   Charters

are nowhere else in the world an expression of popular thought as much as in America. They are merely what people believe or permit at any given period. Very often they are well adapted to our needs, like the late New York charter, but fail to give satisfaction, because, having provided the charter, we take no pains to secure competent officials. Finding that it does not work well, we seek a remedy by making a change in its provisions rather than in the men who administer it. In this way our municipal woes are perpetuated, and we continue to write and talk of charters as if they were self-acting machines, instead of certain ways of doing business. No municipal reform will last long or prove efficient without a strong and healthy public spirit behind it. With this almost any charter would prove efficient.

THE GROWTH AND EXPRESSION OF
PUBLIC OPINION

PUBLIC opinion, like democracy itself, is a
new power which has come into the world since
the Middle Ages. In fact, it is safe to say that
before the French Revolution nothing of the
kind was known or dreamt of in Europe. There
was a certain truth in Louis XIV.'s statement,
which now sounds so droll, that he was himself
the state. Public opinion was *his* opinion. In
England, it may be said with equal safety, there
was nothing that could be called public opinion,
in the modern sense, before the passage of the
Reform Bill. It began to form itself slowly
after 1816. Sir Robert Peel was forced to remark in a letter to Croker in March, 1820: —

"Do you not think that the tone of England,
of that great compound of folly, weakness, prejudice, wrong feeling, right feeling, obstinacy,
or newspaper paragraphs, which is called public
opinion, is more liberal — to use an odious but
intelligible phrase — than the policy of the
government? Do not you think that there is a
feeling becoming daily more general and more

confirmed — that is independent of the pressure
of taxation, or any immediate cause — in favor
of some undefined change in the mode of governing the country? It seems to me a curious
crisis, when public opinion never had such influence in public measures, and yet never was so
dissatisfied with the share which it possessed.
It is growing too large for the channels that it
has been accustomed to run through. God
knows it is very difficult to widen them equally
in proportion to the size and force of the current
which they have to convey, but the engineers
that made them never dreamed of various streams
that are now struggling for vent."

In short, Peel perceived the growth of the
force, and he recognized it as a new force. In
America public opinion can hardly be said to
have existed before the Revolution. The opinions of leading men, of clergymen and large
landholders, were very powerful, and settled
most of the affairs of state; but the opinion of
the majority did not count for much, and the
majority, in truth, did not think that it should.
In other words, public opinion had not been
created. It was the excitement of the Revolutionary War which brought it into existence,
and made it seem omnipotent. It is obvious,
however, that there are two kinds of public
opinion. One kind is the popular belief in the

fitness or rightness of something, which Mr.
Balfour calls "climate," a belief that certain
lines of conduct should be followed, or a certain
opinion held, by good citizens, or right-thinking
persons.   Such a belief does not impose any
duty on anybody beyond outward conformity to
the received standards.   The kind I am now
talking of is the public opinion, or consensus of
opinion, among large bodies of persons, which
acts as a political force, imposing on those in
authority certain legislation, or certain lines of
policy.   The first of these does not change, and
is not seriously modified in much less than fifty
years.   The second is being incessantly modified
by the events of the day.

All the writers on politics are agreed as to the
influence which this latter public opinion ought
to have on government.   They all acknowledge
that in modern constitutional states it ought to
be omnipotent.   It is in deciding from what
source it should come that the democrats and
the aristocrats part company.   According to the
aristocratic school, it should emanate only from
persons possessing a moderate amount of property, on the assumption that the possession of
property argues some degree of intelligence and
interest in public affairs.   According to the
democratic school, it should emanate from the
majority of the adult males, on the assumption

that it is only in this way that legislators can be made to consult the greatest good of the greatest number, and that, in the long run, the majority of adult males are pretty sure to be right about public questions. President Lincoln came near defining this theory when he said, " You can fool part of the people all the time, and all the people part of the time, but you cannot fool all the people all the time." This probably meant that under the democratic system public opinion forms slowly, and has to be clarified by prolonged discussion, but that it is sure to prove correct eventually.

What appears most to concern us in the tendencies of democratic government is not so much the quality of public opinion, as the way in which it exercises its power over the conduct of affairs. I was struck recently by a remark in a private letter, that " public opinion is as sound as ever, but that the politicians "— that is, the men in control of affairs — " pay just as little attention to it as ever." There is an assumption here that we can get at public opinion in some other way than through elections; that is, that we may know what the public thinks on any particular question, without paying attention to what men in power, who seek to obey the political will, do or say, as a condition of their popular existence. Is this true of any demo-

cratic country? Is it true, in particular, of the
United States of America?

There are only two ways in which public
opinion upon political questions finds expression,
or is thought to find it. One is the vote at
elections, the other is journalism. But public
opinion declares itself through elections only at
intervals of greater or less length: in England,
once in five or six years; in America, once in
two years, or at most in four; in France, once
in four years. It is only at these periods that
public opinion must be sought; at others, it is
consulted at the will of the minister or sovereign,
and he rarely consults it when he can help it, if
he thinks that its decision will be against him,
and that the result will be a loss of power. The
imperfection of elections, however, as a means
of making public opinion known, is very obvious. It is seldom, indeed, that a definite issue
is submitted to the public, like the Swiss referendum, and that the voters are asked to say yes
or no, in answer to a particular question. As
a rule, it is the general policy of the party in
power, on all sorts of subjects, which appears to
determine the action of the voters. The bulk
of them, on both sides, vote for their own party
in any event, no matter what course it has pursued, on the principle that if what it has done
in a particular case is not right, it was as nearly

right as circumstances would permit.   The rem-
nant, or "independents," who turn the scale to
one side or the other, have half a dozen reasons
for their course, or, in other words, express by
their vote their opinions on half a dozen subjects, besides the one on which the verdict of
the majority is sought.   During the last thirty
years, for instance, in the United States, it would
have been almost useless to consult the voters
on any subject except the tariff.   No matter
what question might have been put to them, it
would almost surely have been answered with
reference mainly to the effect of the answer on
the tariff.   All other matters would have been
passed over.   In like manner, it has probably
been impossible in England, for ten or twelve
years, to get a real expression of opinion on any
subject except Irish home rule.   To the inquiry
what people thought about the Armenian mas-
sacres, or education, or liquor regulation, the
voters were pretty sure to answer, "We are opposed to Irish home rule."   Accordingly, after
every election there are disputes as to what it
means.   The defeated party seldom acknowledges that its defeat has been due to the matters
on which the other side claims a victory.
The great triumph of the Conservatives in 1894
was ascribed by them to home rule, but by the
Liberals to local option and clerical hostility

to the common schools. Similarly, the Republican defeat in America in 1890 was due, according to one party, to the excesses of the McKinley tariff, and, according to the other, to gross deceptions practiced on the voters as to its probable effect on prices.

What are called " electioneering devices " or " tricks " are largely based on this uncertainty. That is, they are meant to influence the voters by some sort of matter irrelevant to the main issue. This is called " drawing a red herring across the scent." A good example of it is to be found in the practice, which has prevailed during nearly the whole tariff agitation, of citing the rage, or disgust, or misery of foreigners due to our legislation, as a reason for persisting in it, — as if any legislation which produced this effect on foreigners must be good. But, obviously, there might be much legislation which would excite the hostility of foreigners, and be at the same time injurious to this country. In voting on the tariff, a large number of voters — the Irish for instance — might be, and doubtless were, influenced in favor of high duties by the fact that, to a large extent, they would exclude British goods, and thus they appeared to be approving a protective policy in general. Nobody believes that in Germany the increasing Socialist vote represents Socialist ideas, properly so called. It expresses discontent generally with the existing régime. In Ireland, too, the vote at a general election does not express simply an opinion on the question which has dissolved Parliament. Rather, it expresses general hostility to English rule. In Italy, elections mostly turn on the question of the temporal power of the Pope. In fact, wherever we look at the modes of obtaining expressions of public opinion, we find that elections are not often reliable as to particular measures, except through the referendum. In all democratic countries, it is the practice of the bulk of the voters to indicate by their votes their confidence in, or distrust of, the party in power, rather than their opinions on any particular measure. It is the few who turn the scale who are really influenced by the main question before the voters. The rest follow their party prepossessions, or rely on the party managers to turn the majority, if they secure it, to proper account.

In England, some reliance is placed on what are called "bye elections," — or elections caused by vacancies occurring between two general elections, — as indications of the trend of public opinion touching the acts or policy of the ministry. But these elections very seldom show more than slight diminution or slight increase of preceding majorities, and the result, as an instruction, is very often made uncertain by local causes, such as the greater or less popularity of one of the candidates. They may, and generally do, reveal the growing or declining popularity of the party in power in the constituency in which they occur, but rarely can be held to express the opinion of the majority on any particular matter. There are several ways of accounting for any changes which have occurred in the total vote, all equally plausible. In America, town or county elections serve somewhat the same purpose. They are watched, not so much with reference to their influence on local affairs, as with reference to the light they throw on the feelings of the voters toward the administration for the time being. It is taken for granted that no local wants or incidents will prevent the bulk of the voters from casting their ballots as members of federal parties.

It is probably this disposition to vote on the general course of the administration, rather than on any particular proposal, which causes what it is now the fashion to call the " swinging of the pendulum," — that is, the tendency both in England and in America to vote in a different way at alternate elections, or never to give any party more than one term in power. If public attention were apt to be concentrated on one measure, this could hardly occur so frequently.

It doubtless indicates, not positive condemnation of any particular thing, so much as disapproval or weariness of certain marked features of the government policy. The voters get tired both of praise and of blame of particular men, and so resolve to try others; or they get tired of a certain policy, and long for something new. It is a little difficult to fix on the exact cause of such changes, but it seems pretty certain that they cannot be considered definite expressions of opinion on specific subjects. Then, owing to the electoral divisions through which every country chooses legislators, a far greater change may often be made in the legislature than the vote in the separate constituencies warrants. For instance, a President may readily be chosen in the United States by a minority of the popular vote; and in England, an enormous majority in the House of Commons may rest on a very small aggregate majority of the electors. There never was a more striking illustration of the difficulty of getting at popular opinion than the defeat of the Disraeli ministry in 1880. It was the confident belief of all the more instructed portion of the community — the gentry, the clergy, and the professional class — that, rightly or wrongly, public opinion was on the side of the ministry, and approved what was called its "imperial policy," — the provocation given to Afghanistan, and the interference in the Russo-Turkish war on the side of Turkey. One heard, it was said, nothing else in the clubs, the trains, the hotels, and the colleges. But the result showed that these indications were of little value, that the judgment of the classes most occupied in observing political tendencies was at fault, and that the bulk of the constituencies had apparently taken quite a different view of the whole matter.

A striking example of the same thing was afforded in the State of New York in 1892. The leaders of the Democratic party at that time were men of more than usual astuteness and political experience. It was of the last importance to them to learn the popular judgment on the more recent acts of the party, particularly on the mode in which it had secured control of the state Senate. Up to the day of election they seem to have had the utmost confidence in an overwhelming popular verdict in their favor. The result, however, was their overwhelming defeat. They apparently had but a very slight knowledge of the trend of public opinion. In truth, it may be said that the great political revolutions wrought by elections, both in England and in America, have been unexpected by the bulk of observers, either wholly or as to their extent. No change at all was looked for, or the change was not expected to be so great.

Why this should be so, why in a democratic society people should find so much difficulty in discovering beforehand what the sovereign power is thinking, and what it is going to do, is not so difficult to explain as it seems. We must first bear in mind that the democratic societies prodigiously increased in size almost at the moment at which they acquired control of the State. There was no previous opportunity for examining their tastes, prejudices, weaknesses, or tendencies. Most of the descriptions of democracies within the present century, as I have already pointed out, have been only guesses, or deductions from the history of those of antiquity. Nearly every modern writer on this subject has fallen into mistakes about democratic tendencies, merely through à *priori* reasoning. Certain things had happened in the ancient democracies, and were sure to happen again in the modern democracies, much as the conditions had changed. Singularly enough, the one absolutely new difficulty, the difficulty of consulting a modern democracy, has hardly been noticed. This difficulty has produced the boss, who is a sufficiently simple phenomenon. But how, without the boss, to get at what the people are thinking, has not been found out, though it is of great importance. We have not yet hit on the best plan of getting at " public opinion."

Elections, as we have seen, are the medium through which this force manifests itself in action, but they do not furnish the reason of this action, the considerations which led to it, or a forecast of all the consequences it is expected to produce. Moreover, at best they tell us only what half the people are thinking ; for no party nowadays wins an electoral victory by much over half the voters. So that we are driven back, for purposes of observation, on the newspaper press.

Our confidence in this is based on the theory, not so much that the newspapers make public opinion, as that the opinions they utter are those of which their readers approve. But this ground is being made less tenable every year by the fact that more and more newspapers rely on advertising, rather than on subscriptions, for their support and profits, and agreement with their readers is thus less and less important to them. The old threat of " stopping my paper," if a subscriber came across unpalatable views in the editorial columns, is therefore not so formidable as it used to be, and is less resorted to. The advertiser, rather than the subscriber, is now the newspaper bogie. He is the person before whom the publisher cowers and whom he tries to please, and the advertiser is very indifferent about the opinions of a newspaper. What interests him is the amount or quality of its circu-

lation.   What he wants to know is, how many
and what class of persons see it, not how many
persons agree with it.   The consequence is that
the newspapers of largest circulation, published
in the great centres of population where most
votes are cast, are less and less organs of opinion, especially in America.   In fact, in some
cases the advertisers use their influence — which
is great, and which the increasing competition
between newspapers makes all the greater — to
prevent the expression in newspapers of what is
probably the prevailing local view of men or
events.   There are not many newspapers which
can afford to defy a large advertiser.

Nothing is more striking in the reading public to-day, in our democracy, than the increasing
incapacity for continuous attention.   The power
of attention is one that, just like muscular
power, needs cultivation or training.   The ability to listen to a long argument or exposition, or
to read it, involves not only strength but habit
in the muscles of the eye or the nerves of the
ear.   In familiar language, one has to be used
to it, to do it easily.

There seems to be a great deal of reason for
believing that this habit is becoming much rarer.
Publishers complain more and more of the refusal of nearly every modern community to read
books, except novels, which keep the attention

alive by amusing incidents and rapid changes
of situation. Argumentative works can rarely
count on a large circulation. This may doubtless be ascribed in part to the multiplicity of
the objects of attention in modern times, to the
opportunities of simple amusement, to the large
area of the world which is brought under each
man's observation by the telegraph, and to the
general rapidity of communication. But this
large area is brought under observation through
the newspaper ; and that the newspaper's mode
of presenting facts does seriously affect the way
in which people perform the process called
" making up their minds," especially about public questions, can hardly be denied. The nearest approach we can make to what people are
thinking about any matter of public interest is
undoubtedly by " reading the papers." It may
not be a sure way, but there is no other. It is
true, often lamentably true, that the only idea
most foreigners and observers get of a nation's
modes of thought and standards of duty and
excellence, and in short of its manners and
morals, comes through reading its periodicals.
To the outsider the newspaper press is the nation talking about itself. Nations are known
to other nations mainly through their press.
They used to be known more by their public
men ; but the class of public men who repre-

sent a country is becoming every day smaller,
and public men speak less than formerly; with
us they can scarcely be said to speak at all. Our
present system of nomination and the loss of
the habit of debating in the legislature, have
almost put an end to oratory, except during exciting canvasses. Elsewhere than in England,
the names of the leading men are hardly known
to foreigners; their utterances, not at all. If I
want to learn the drift of opinion in any country, on any topic, the best thing I can do, therefore, is to read the papers; and I must read a
large number.

In America more than in any other country,
the collection of " news " has become a business
within half a century, and it has been greatly
promoted by the improvements in the printing-
press. Before this period, "news" was generally news of great events, — that is, of events
of more than local importance; so that if a man
were asked, " What news?" he would try, in
his answer, to mention something of world-wide
significance. But as soon as the collection of
it became a business, submitted to the ordinary
laws of competition, the number of things that
were called " news " naturally increased. Each
newspaper endeavored to outdo its rivals by the
greater number of facts it brought to the public
notice, and it was not very long before " news "

became everything whatever, no matter how unimportant, which the reader had not previously
heard of.   The sense of proportion about news
was rapidly destroyed.   Everything, however
trifling, was considered worth printing, and the
newspaper finally became, what it is now, a collection of the gossip, not only of the whole world,
but of its own locality.   Now, gossip, when
analyzed, consists simply of a collection of actual
facts, mostly of little moment, and also of sur-
mises about things, of equally little moment.
But business requires that as much importance
as possible shall be given to them by the manner
of producing each item, or what is called " typo-
graphical display."   Consequently they are presented with separate and conspicuous headings,
and there is no necessary connection between
them.   They follow one another, column after
column, without any order, either of subject or
of chronology.

The diligent newspaper reader, therefore, gets
accustomed to passing rapidly from one to another of a series of incidents, small and great,
requiring simply the transfer, from one trifle to
another, of a sort of lazy, uninterested attention, which often becomes sub-conscious ; that
is, a man reads with hardly any knowledge or
recollection of what he is reading.   Not only
does the attention become habituated to frequent

breaches in its continuity, but it grows accustomed to short paragraphs, as one does to passers-by in the street. A man sees and observes them, but does not remember what he sees and observes for more than a minute or two. That this should have its effect on the editorial writing is what naturally might be expected. If the editorial article is long, the reader, used to the short paragraphs, is apt to shrink from the labor of perusing it; if it is brief, he pays little more attention to it than he pays to the paragraphs. When, therefore, any newspaper turns to serious discussion in its columns, it is difficult, and one may say increasingly difficult, to get a hearing. It has to contend both against the intellectual habit of its readers, which makes prolonged attention hard, and against *à priori* doubts of its honesty and competency. People question whether it is talking in good faith, or has some sinister object in view, knowing that in one city of the Union, at least, it is impossible to get published any criticism on the larger advertisers, however nefarious their doings; knowing also that in another city there have been rapid changes of journalistic views, made for party purposes or through simple changes of ownership.

The result is that the effect of newspaper editorial writing on opinion is small, so far as one can judge. Still, it would be undeniably large enough to possess immense power if the press acted unanimously as a body. If all the papers, or a great majority of them, said the same thing on any question of the day, or told the same story about any matter in dispute, they would undoubtedly possess great influence. But they are much divided, partly by political affiliation, and partly, perhaps mainly, by business rivalry. For business purposes, each is apt to think it necessary to differ in some degree from its nearest rivals, whether of the same party or not, in its view of most questions, or at all events not to support a rival's view, or totally to ignore something to which the rival is attaching great importance. The result is that the press rarely acts with united force, or expresses a united opinion. Nor do many readers subscribe to more than one paper; and consequently few readers have any knowledge of the other side of any question on which their own paper is, possibly, preaching with vehemence. The great importance which many persons attach to having a newspaper of large circulation on their side is due in some degree to its power in the presentation of facts to the public, and also to its power of annoyance by persistent abuse or ridicule.

Another agency which has interfered with the press as an organ of opinion is the greatly

increased expense of starting or carrying on a
modern newspaper.   The days when Horace
Greeley or William Lloyd Garrison could start
an influential paper in a small printing-office,
with the assistance of a boy, are gone forever.
Few undertakings require more capital, or are
more hazardous.   The most serious item of expense is the collection of news from all parts of
the world, and this cannot be evaded in our day.
News is the life-blood of the modern newspaper.
No talent or energy will make up for its absence.   The consequence is that a very large
sum is needed to establish a newspaper.   After
it is started, a large sum must be spent without
visible return, but the fortune that may be ac-
cumulated by it, if successful, is also very large.
One of the most curious things about it is that
the public does not expect from a newspaper
proprietor the same sort of morality that it ex-
pects from persons in other callings.   It would
disown a bookseller and cease all intercourse with
him for a tithe of the falsehoods and petty
frauds which it passes unnoticed in a newspaper
proprietor.   It may disbelieve every word he
says, and yet profess to respect him, and may
occasionally reward him; so that it is quite possible to find a newspaper which nearly everybody
condemns, and whose influence most men would
repudiate, circulating very freely even among

religious and moral people, and making handsome profits. A newspaper proprietor, therefore, who finds that his profits remain high, no matter what views he promulgates and what kind of morality he practices, can hardly, with fairness to the community, be treated as an exponent of its opinions. He will not consider what it thinks, when he finds he has only to consider what it will buy, and that it will buy his paper without agreeing with it.

But it is as an exponent of the nation's feeling about other nations that the press is most defective. The old diplomacy, in which, as Disraeli said, "sovereigns and statesmen" regulated international affairs in secret conclave in gorgeous salons, has all but passed away. The "sovereigns and statesmen" and the secret conclave and the gorgeous salons remain, but of the old indifference to what the world outside thought of their work, not very much remains. Now and then a king or an emperor gratifies his personal spites, in his instructions to his diplomatic representatives, like the Emperor of Germany in the case of the unfortunate Greeks; but most governments, in their negotiations with foreign powers, now listen closely to the voice of their own people. The democracy sits at every council board, and the most conservative of ministers, consciously or unconsciously, con-

sults it as well as he can. He tries to find out
what it wishes in any particular matter, or, if
this be impossible, he tries to find out what will
most impress its imagination. Whether he
brings peace or war, he tries to make it appear
that the national honor has been carefully looked
after, and that the national desires, and even the
national weaknesses, have been considered and
provided for. But it is from the press that he
must learn all this; and it is from the press, too,
that each diplomatist must learn whether his
opponent's country is really behind him. The
press is never silent, and it has the field to itself;
any one who wishes to know what the people
are feeling and thinking has to rely on it for the
want of anything better.

In international questions, however, the press
is often a poor reliance. In the first place,
business prudence prompts an editor, whether
he fully understands the matter under discussion
or not, to take what seems the patriotic view;
and tradition generally makes the selfish, quar-
relsome view the patriotic view. The late editor
of the "Sun" expressed this tersely by advising
young journalists "always to stand by the Stars
and Stripes." It was long ago expressed still
more tersely by the cry, "Our country, right
or wrong!" All first-class Powers still live
more or less openly, in their relations with one

another, under the old dueling code, which the
enormous armaments in modern times render
almost a necessity. Under this code the one
unbearable imputation is fear of somebody.
Any other imputation a nation supports with
comparative meekness; the charge of timidity
is intolerable. It has been made more so by
the conversion of most modern nations into
great standing armies, and no great standing
army can for a moment allow the world to doubt
its readiness, and even eagerness, to fight. It
is not every diplomatic difference that is at first
clearly understood by the public. Very often
the pros and cons of the matter are imperfectly
known until the correspondence is published,
but the agitation of the popular mind continues;
the press must talk about the matter, and its
talk is rarely pacific. It is bound by tradition
to take the ground that its own government is
right; and that even if it is not, it does not
make any difference, — the press has to maintain
that it is right.

The action of Congress on the recent Vene-
zuelan complication well illustrated the position
of the press in such matters. When Mr. Cleveland sent his message asking Congress to vote
the expense of tracing the frontier of a foreign
power, Congress knew nothing of the merits of
the case. It did not even know that any such

controversy was pending. As the message was distinctly one that might lead to war, and as Congress was the war-making power, the Constitution presumptively imposed on it the duty of examining the causes of the dispute thoroughly, before complying with the President's request. In most other affairs, too, it would have been the more disposed to discharge this duty, because the majority was hostile to Mr. Cleveland. But any delay or hesitation, it feared, would be construed by the public as a symptom of fear or of want of patriotism, so it instantly voted the money without any examination whatever. The press was in an almost similar condition. It knew no more of the merits of the case than Congress, and it had the same fear of being thought wanting in patriotism, so that the whole country in twenty-four hours resounded with rhetorical preparation for, and justification of, war with England.

As long as this support is confined to argumentation, no great harm is done. The diplomatists generally care but little about the dialectical backing up that they get from the newspapers. Either they do not need it, or it is too ill informed to do them much good. But the newspapers have another concern than mere victory in argument. They have to maintain their place in the estimation of their readers, and, if possible, to increase the number of these readers. Unhappily, in times of international trouble, the easiest way to do this always *seems* to be to influence the public mind against the foreigner. This is done partly by impugning his motives in the matter in hand, and partly by painting his general character in an odious light. Undoubtedly this produces some effect on the public mind by begetting a readiness to punish in arms, at any cost, so unworthy an adversary. The worst effect, however, is that which is produced on the ministers conducting the negotiations. It frightens or encourages them into taking extreme positions, in putting forward impossible claims, or in perverting history and law to help their case. The applause and support of the newspapers seem to be public opinion. They bring honor at home, no matter how the controversy ends. In short, it may be said, as a matter of history, that in few diplomatic controversies in this century has the press failed to make moderate ground difficult for a diplomatist, and retreats from untenable positions almost impossible. The press makes his case seem so good, that abandonment of it looks like treason to his country.

Then there is another aspect of the case which cannot be passed without notice, though it puts the press in a less honorable light. Newspapers

are made to sell; and for this purpose there is
nothing better than war. War means daily sensation and excitement. On this almost any kind
of newspaper may live and make money. Whether
the war brings victory or defeat makes little difference. The important thing is that in war
every moment may bring important and exciting
news, — news which does not need to be accurate
or to bear sifting. What makes it most market-
able is that it is probable and agreeable, although
disagreeable news sells nearly as well. In the
tumult of a great war, when the rules of evidence are suspended by passion or anxiety, invention, too, is easy, and has its value, and is pretty
sure never to be punished. Some newspapers,
which found it difficult to make a livelihood in
times of peace, made fortunes in our last war;
and it may be said that, as a rule, troublous times
are the best for a newspaper proprietor.

It follows from this, it cannot but follow,
that it is only human for a newspaper proprietor
to desire war, especially when he feels sure that
his own country is right, and that its opponents
are enemies of civilization, — a state of mind
into which a man may easily work himself by
writing and talking much during an international controversy. So that I do not think it an
exaggeration or a calumny to say that the press,
taken as a whole, — of course with many honor-

able exceptions, — has a bias in favor of war.
It would not stir up a war with any country, but
if it sees preparations made to fight, it does not
fail to encourage the combatants. This is particularly true of a naval war, which is much more
striking as a spectacle than a land war, while it
does not disturb industry or distribute personal
risk, to nearly the same extent.

Of much more importance, however, than the
manner in which public opinion finds expression
in a democracy is the manner in which it is
formed, and this is very much harder to get at.
I do not mean what may be called people's standing opinion about things in general, which is
born of hereditary prejudice, and works itself
into the manners of the country as part of each
individual's moral and intellectual outfit. There
is a whole batch of notions about things public
and private, which men of every nation hold because they are national, — once called " Roman "
by a Roman, now " English " by an Englishman,
and " American " by an American, — and which
are defended or propagated simply by calling
the opposite " un-English " or " un-American."
These views come to people by descent. They
are inherited rather than formed. What I have
in mind is the opinions formed by the community
about new subjects, questions of legislation and
of war and peace, and about social needs or sins

or excesses, — in short, about anything novel, which calls imperatively for an immediate judgment of some kind. What is it that moves large bodies or parties in a democracy like ours, for instance, to say that its government should do this, or should not do that, in any matter that may happen to be before them?

Nothing can be more difficult than an answer to this question. Every writer about democracy, from Montesquieu down, has tried to answer it by *à priori* predictions as to what democracy will say, or do, or think, under certain given circumstances. The uniform failure naturally suggests the conclusion that the question is not answerable at all, owing largely to the enormously increased number of influences under which all men act in the modern world. It is now very rare to meet with one of the distinctly defined characters which education, conducted under the régime of authority, used to form, down to the close of the last century. There are really no more " divines," or " gentlemen," or " Puritans," or "John Bulls," or "Brother Jonathans." In other words, there are no more moral or intellectual moulds. It used to be easy to say how a given individual or community would look at a thing; at present it is well-nigh impossible. We can hardly tell what agency is exercising the strongest influence on popular thought on any given occasion. Most localities and classes are subject to some peculiar dominating force, but if you discover what it is, you discover it almost by accident. One of the latest attempts to define a moral force that would be sure to act on opinion was the introduction into the political arena in England of the " Nonconformist conscience," or the moral training of the dissenting denominations, — Congregationalists, Methodists, and Baptists. In the discussion of Irish home rule and various cognate matters, much use has been made of the *term*, but it is difficult to point to any particular occasion in which the *thing* has distinctly made itself felt. One would have said, twenty years ago, that the English class of country squires would be the last body in the world, owing to temperament and training, to approve of any change in the English currency. We believe they are to-day largely bimetallists. The reason is that their present liabilities, contracted in good times, have been made increasingly heavy by the fall in agricultural produce.

The same phenomena are visible here in America. It would be difficult to-day to say what is the American opinion, properly so called, about the marriage bond. One would think that in the older states, in which social life is more settled, it would strongly favor indissolubility, or, at all events, great difficulty of dissolution. But this is not the case. In Connecticut and Rhode Island divorce is as easy, and almost as little disreputable, as in any of the newer Western states. In the discussion on the currency, most observers would have predicted that the power of the government over its value would be most eagerly preached by the states in which the number of foreign voters was greatest. As a matter of fact, these states proved at the election to be the firmest friends of the gold standard. Within our own lifetime the Southern or cotton states, from being very conservative, have become very radical, in the sense of being ready to give ear to new ideas. What we might have said of them in 1860 would be singularly untrue in 1900. One might go over the civilized world in this way, and find that the public opinion of each country, on any given topic, had escaped from the philosophers, so to speak, — that all generalizing about it had become difficult, and that it was no longer possible to divide influences into categories.

The conclusion most readily reached about the whole matter is that authority, whether in religion or in morals, which down to the last century was so powerful, has ceased to exert much influence on the affairs of the modern world, and that any attempt to mould opinion on religious or moral or political questions, by

its instrumentality, is almost certain to prove
futile.   The reliance of the older political
writers, from Grotius to Locke, on the sayings
of other previous writers or on the Bible, is now
among the curiosities of literature.   Utilitarian-
ism, however we may feel about it, has fully
taken possession of political discussion.   That is
to say, any writer or speaker on political subjects
has to show that his proposition will make people more comfortable or richer.   This is tanta-
mount to saying that historic experience has not
nearly the influence on political affairs it once
had.   The reason is obvious.   The number of
persons who have something to say about political affairs has increased a thousandfold, but the
practice of reading books has not increased, and
it is in books that experience is recorded.   In
the past, the governing class, in part at least,
was a reading class.   One of the reasons which
are generally said to have given the Southern
members special influence in Congress before the
war is that they read books, had libraries, and
had wide knowledge of the experiments tried by
earlier generations of mankind.   Their successors rarely read anything but the newspapers.
This is increasingly true, also, of other democratic countries.   The old literary type of
statesmen, of which Jefferson and Madison and
Hamilton, Guizot and Thiers, were examples,

is rapidly disappearing, if it has not already disappeared.

The importance of this in certain branches of public affairs is great, — the management of currency, for example. All we know about currency we learn from the experience of the human race. What man will do about any kind of money, — gold, silver, or paper, — under any given set of conditions, we can predict only by reading of what man has done. What will happen, if, of two kinds of currency, we lower or raise the value of one, what will happen if we issue too much irredeemable paper, why we must make our paper redeemable, what are the dangers of violent and sudden changes in the standard of value, are all things which we can ascertain only from the history of money. What any man now thinks or desires about the matter is of little consequence compared with what men in times past have tried to do. The loss of influence or weight by the reading class is therefore of great importance, for to this loss we undoubtedly owe most of the prevalent wild theories about currency. They are the theories of men who do not know that their experiments have been tried already and have failed. In fact, I may almost venture the assertion that the influence of history on politics was never smaller than it is to-day, although history was never before cultivated with so much acumen and industry. So that authority and experience may fairly be ruled out of the list of forces which seriously influence the government of democratic societies. In the formation of public opinion they do not greatly count.

The effect of all this is not simply to lead to hasty legislation. It also has an injurious effect on legislative decision, in making every question seem an " open " or " large " question. As nothing, or next to nothing, is settled, all problems of politics have a tendency to seem new to every voter, — matters of which each man is as good a judge as another, and as much entitled to his own opinion. He is likely to consider himself under no special obligation to agree with anybody else. The only obligation he feels is that of party, and this is imposed to secure victories at the polls, rather than to insure any particular kind of legislation. For instance, a man may be a civil service reformer when the party takes no action about it, or a gold man when the party rather favors silver, or a free-trader when the party advocates high tariff, and yet be a good party man as long as he votes the ticket. He may question all the opinions in its platform, but if he thinks it is the best party to administer the government or distribute the offices, he may and does remain in it with perfect comfort. In short, party discipline does not insure uniformity of opinion, but simply uniformity of action at election.   The platform is not held to impose any line of action on the voters.   Neither party in America to-day has any fixed creed.   Every voter believes what is good in his own eyes, and may do so with impunity, without loss of party standing, as long as he votes for the party nominee at every important election.

The pursuit of any policy in legislation is thus, undoubtedly, more difficult than of old. The phrase, well known to lawyers, that a thing is " against public policy," has by no means the same meaning now that it once had, for it is very difficult to say what " public policy " is. National policy is something which has to be committed to the custody of a few men who respect tradition and are familiar with records. A large assembly which is not dominated by a leader, and in which each member thinks he knows as much as any other member, and does not study or respect records, can hardly follow a policy without a good deal of difficulty.   The disappearance from the governments of the United States, France, and Italy of commanding figures, whose authority or character imposed on minor men, accordingly makes it hard to say what is the policy of these three countries on most questions.   Ministers who do not carry

personal weight always seek to fortify themselves
by the conciliation of voters, and what will conciliate voters is, under every democratic régime,
a matter of increasing uncertainty, so free is the
play of individual opinion.

Of this, again, the condition of our currency
question at this moment is a good illustration.
Twenty-five years ago, the custody and regulation of the standard of value, like the custody
and regulation of the standard of length or of
weight, were confided to experts, without objection in any quarter. There was no more thought
of disputing with these experts about it than of
disputing with mathematicians or astronomers
about problems in their respective sciences. It
was not thought that there could be a " public
opinion " about the comparative merits of the
metals as mediums of exchange, any more than
about the qualities of triangles or the position
of stars. The experts met now and then, in
private conclave, and decided, without criticism
from any one else, whether silver or gold should
be the legal tender. All the public asked was
that the standard, whatever it was, should be the
steadiest possible, the least liable to fluctuations
or variations.

With the growing strength of the democratic
régime all this has been changed. The standard
of value, like nearly everything else about which

men are concerned, has descended into the political arena. Every man claims the right to have an opinion about it, as good as that of any other man. More than this, nearly every man is eager to get this opinion embodied in legislation if he can. Nobody is listened to by all as an authority on the subject. The most eminent financiers find their views exposed to nearly as much question as those of any tyro. The idea that money should be a standard of value, as good as the nature of value will permit, has almost disappeared. Money has become a means in the hands of governments of alleviating human misery, of lightening the burdens of unfortunate debtors, and of stimulating industry. On the best mode of doing these things, every man thinks he is entitled to his say. The result is that we find ourselves, in the presence of one of the most serious financial problems which has ever confronted any nation, without a financial leader. The finances of the Revolution had Alexander Hamilton, and subsequently Albert Gallatin. The finances of the civil war had first Secretary Chase, and subsequently Senator Sherman, both of whom brought us to some sort of conclusion, if not always to the right conclusion, by sheer weight of authority. To Senator Sherman we were mainly indebted for the return to specie payment in 1879. At present we have no one who fills the places of these men in the public eye. No one assumes to lead in this crisis, though many give good as well as bad advice; but all, or nearly all, who advise, advise as politicians, not as financiers. Very few who speak on the subject say publicly the things they say in private. Their public deliverances are modified or toned down to suit some part of the country, or some set or division of voters. They are what is called "politically wise." During the twenty years following the change in the currency in 1873 no leading man in either party disputed the assertions of the advocates of silver as to the superiority of silver to gold as a standard of value. Nearly all politicians, even of the Republican party, admitted the force of some of the contentions of those advocates, and were willing to meet them halfway, by some such measure as the purchase of silver under the Sherman Act. The result was that when Mr. Bryan was nominated on a silver platform, his followers attacked the gold standard with weapons drawn from the armory of the gold men, and nearly every public man of prominence was estopped from vigorous opposition to them by his own utterances on the same subject.

It is easy to see that under circumstances like these a policy about finance — the most important matter in which a nation can have a policy

— is hardly possible. There are too many opinions in the field for the formation of anything that can be called public opinion. And yet, I cannot recall any case in history, or, in other words, in human experience, in which a great scheme of financial reform was carried through without having some man of force or weight behind it, some man who had framed it, who understood it, who could answer objections to it, and who was not obliged to alter or curtail it against his better judgment. The great financiers stand out in bold relief in the financial chronicles of every nation. They may have been wrong, they may have made mistakes, but they spoke imperiously and carried their point, whatever it was.

Whether the disposition to do without them, and to control money through popular opinion, which seems now to have taken possession of the democratic world, will last, or whether it will be abandoned after trial, remains to be seen. But one is not a rash prophet who predicts that it will fail. Finance is too full of details, of unforeseen effects, of technical conditions, to make the mastery of it possible, without much study and experience. There is no problem of government which comes so near being strictly "scientific," that is, so dependent on principles of human nature and so little dependent on legislative power. No government can completely control the medium of exchange. It is a subject for psychology rather than for politics. Democracy has apparently been taken possession of by the idea, either that a perfect standard of value may be contrived, or that the standard of value may be made a philanthropic instrument. But in view of the incessant and rapid change of cost of production which everything undergoes in this age of invention and discovery, gold and silver included, the idea of a perfect standard of value must be set down as a chimera. Every one acknowledges this. What some men maintain is that the effects of invention and discovery may be counteracted by law and even by treaty, which is simply an assertion that parliaments and congresses and diplomatists can determine what each man shall give for everything he buys. This proposition hardly needs more than a statement of it for its refutation. It is probably the most unexpected of all the manifestations of democratic feeling yet produced. For behind all proposals to give currency a legal value differing from the value of the marketplace lies a belief in the strength of law such as the world has never yet seen. All previous régimes have believed in the power of law to enforce physical obedience, and to say what shall constitute the legal payment of a debt, but never until now has it been maintained that government can create the standard of value, that is, create in each head the amount of desire which fixes the price of a commodity.

In short, the one thing which can be said with most certainty about democratic public opinion in the modern world is that it is moulded as never before by economic, rather than by religious, or moral, or political considerations. The influences which governed the world down to the close of the seventeenth century were respect for a reigning family, or belief in a certain form of religious worship and horror of others, or national pride and corresponding dislike or distrust of foreigners, or commercial rivalry. It is only the last which has now much influence on public opinion or in legislation. There is not much respect, that can be called a political force, left for any reigning family. There is a general indifference to all forms of religious worship, or at least sufficient indifference to prevent strong or combative attachment to them. Religious wars are no longer possible; the desire to spread any form of faith by force of arms, which so powerfully influenced the politics of the sixteenth and seventeenth centuries, has completely disappeared. It is only in Spain and in Turkey that this feeling can now be said to exist as a power in the state.

The growth of indifference to what used to be called political liberty, too, has been curiously rapid. Political liberty, as the term was understood at the beginning of this century, was the power of having something to say in the election of all officers of the state, and through them of influencing legislation and administration ; or, in other words, of enforcing strict responsibility for its acts on the part of the governing body towards the people. There is apparently much less importance attached to this now than formerly, as is shown by the surrender of the power of nomination to " the bosses " in so many states; and in New York by the growing readiness to pass legislation without debate under direction from the outside. Similarly, socialism, which seems to be the political creed which has strongest hold on the working classes to-day, is essentially a form of domination over the whole individual by the constituted authorities, without consulting him. The only choice left him is one of an occupation, and of the kind of food he will eat and the kind of clothes he will wear. As there is to be no war, no money, no idleness, and no taxation, there will be no politics, and consequently no discussion. In truth, the number of men who would hail such a form of society with delight, as relieving them from all anxiety about sustenance, and from all need of skill or character, is probably large and increasing. For similar reasons, the legislation which excites most attention is apt to be legislation which in some way promises an increase of physical comfort. It is rarely, for instance, that a trades union or workingman's association shows much interest in any law except one which promises to increase wages, or shorten hours of labor, or lower fares or the price of something. Protection, to which a very large number of workingmen are attached, is only in their eyes a mode of keeping wages up. "Municipal ownership" is another name for low fares; restrictions on immigration are a mode of keeping competitors out of the labor market.

All these things, and things of a similar nature, attract a great deal of interest; the encroachments of the bosses on constitutional government, comparatively little. The first attempt to legislate for the economical benefit of the masses was the abolition of the English corn laws. It may seem at first sight that the enactment of the corn laws was an economical measure. But such was not the character in which the corn laws were originally advocated. They were called for, first, in order to make England self-supporting in case of a war with foreign powers, a contingency which was constantly present to men's minds in the last century; secondly, to keep up the country gentry, or "landed interest," as it was called, which then had great political value and importance. The abolition of these laws was avowedly carried out simply for the purpose of cheapening and enlarging the loaf. It was the beginning of a series of measures in various countries which aim merely at increasing human physical comfort, whatever their effect on the structure of the government or on the play of political institutions. This foreshadowed the greatest change which has come over the modern world. It is now governed mainly by ideas about the distribution of commodities. This distribution is not only what most occupies public opinion, but what has most to do with forming it.

THE AUSTRALIAN DEMOCRACY

THE only really democratic experiment, beside our own, going on in the world to-day, is that of the English Australian colonies. All others are more or less disturbed by the political or social traditions of an anterior régime. Nowhere else, therefore, can so much instruction be obtained as to the probable effect of popular government on laws and manners. There is no other democracy whose beginning so nearly resembles ours. We began, it is true, at a much earlier period, under the influence of aristocratic and religious ideas which have lost their force, and we began with a very different class of men. Our first settlers were a selected body, with strong prepossessions in favor of some sort of organization, which, whatever it was to be, was certainly not to be democratic. They sought to reproduce the monarchical or aristocratic world they had left, as far as circumstances would permit. It may fairly be said that the society they tried to establish on this side of the Atlantic was the society of the Old World, with some improvements, notably another kind of established church. By the time the Australian colonies were founded, however, — that is, about a century ago, — what was most antiquated in the American régime had fairly departed. The colonies here had sloughed off a good deal of the European incrustation, and had frankly entered on the democratic régime, but with social foundations such as the Australians could not claim.

Australia originated with New South Wales, and was first settled as a convict station. Most of the earliest emigrants were men transported for crime, and long treated as slaves. The first step taken toward social organization was the bestowal of large tracts of land on English capitalists, to be used as sheep-farms, with the convicts as herdsmen or laborers. Free emigrants came slowly to open up agriculture as a field of industry. As they increased, hostility to the large sheep-farmers was developed in a process somewhat similar to the extinction of the great manors in New York. In fact, New South Wales passed nearly half a century in getting rid of the defects of its foundation, in clarifying its social constitution, and in bringing itself into something like harmony with the other civilized societies of the world. In 1842 the colonies received a legislature, a large proportion of the members of which were nominees of the crown. During the previous half-century they were governed despotically by governors, often broken-down aristocrats, sent out from England. Their society was composed largely of the great sheep-farmers and of actual or emancipated convicts. Religion and morals were for a time at the lowest ebb. The institution of marriage hardly existed. The multitude of female convicts and the thinness of population in the interior, rendered concubinage easy and general. The press had not begun to draw respectable talent from England, and the newspapers, such as they were, were largely in the hands of ex-convicts. There was nothing that could be called public opinion. The only appeal against any wrong-doing lay to the home government, which was then six months away; and so deeply seated was the belief in England that Australia was simply a community of criminals, that any appeals received but little attention.

The first thing that could be called a political party in the colony consisted of Irish Catholic immigrants, who had gone out in large numbers in 1841, under the stimulation of government grants and bounties. They acted rather as Catholics than as citizens, and, as usual, under the leadership of their clergy. A responsible legislature of two houses was not established until 1856. The colonies started with the English, or cabinet system; that is, with ministries selected or approved by Parliament. This was the first great difference between us and them. The framers of the American Constitution decided, for reasons which seemed to them good, to give the executive a definite term of office, independent of legislative approval. This they conceived to be necessary to the establishment of complete independence between the different departments of the government. The separation of the executive, judicial, and legislative branches held a very high place in the minds of all political speculators in the eighteenth century, after Montesquieu had dwelt on its necessity. Therefore, the founders of the American republic made each branch independent in its own sphere, with its own term of office, which the others could neither lengthen nor abridge. This is what is called the presidential system. The cabinet system makes the executive not only part and parcel of the legislative branch, but dependent on it for existence. A vote of the majority can change the executive, while the executive can order a renewal of the legislative branch; that is, dissolve it. The presidential system is undoubtedly the best defense that could be devised against democratic changeableness, or the influence on the government of sudden bursts of popular feeling. But it almost goes to the other extreme. It is very difficult to make any change in public policy or legislation in the United States in less than five years. In Australia, under the cabinet system, six changes may be made in a year. In New South Wales, there have been forty-one ministries, doubtless with entirely different views on important subjects, in thirty-seven years, or more than one change each year. The same phenomena exhibit themselves in all the countries which have adopted the British system, or in which the royal prerogative still remains a legislative force. Unhappily, in the colonies as in France, these frequent changes do not always mean changes of policy. Ministries are too often overthrown simply to satisfy personal rancor, or disappointment, or jealousy.

Another point of difference between our beginning and that of the Australians was that they had no constitution, as we call it; that is, no organic law, paramount to all other laws, and which all legislators were bound to respect in legislating. Every government was organized under an English act of Parliament, but this simply provided a framework, and placed almost no restrictions on the subjects of legislation, because there are no restrictions on the action of the English Parliament itself. The will of Parliament is the British constitution, and the will of the Australian legislatures is the constitution of the colonies, provided they make no attack on the supremacy of the British crown; that is, they may do anything which Parliament may do, provided they obey the imperial law which sets them up. This has some good effects, and some bad ones. It decidedly increases the sense of responsibility, in which our legislatures are so often wanting. The Australians know that any act they pass will be executed, that no intervention of the courts on constitutional grounds can be looked for, and that if the law works badly the action of public sentiment will be immediate, and may lead to the overthrow of the ministry for the time being. In fact, a law paramount, drawn up by picked men, assembling for the purpose at stated intervals of twenty years or less, and safeguarding all the primary social rights against popular passion or impulse or legislative corruption, and interpreted by the courts, is a device peculiar to the United States. It is the only really valid check on democracy ever devised, but it is doubtful whether it could now be set up anywhere else with effect. Its Revolutionary origin has surrounded it with a sanctity which it would be difficult to give any court created in our day and gainsaying the popular will. On the other hand, this absence of constitution gives legislatures a freedom in trying social experiments greater than ours enjoy, though they enjoy a good deal. There is hardly any mode of dealing with private property or private rights which an Australian legislature may not attempt, hardly any experiment in taxation which it may not try. Its sole restraint lies in the quick action of popular reprobation.

These two facts — the adoption of the cabinet system from England, and the absence of a constitution containing restraints on legislation — are the main differences between our democracy and that of Australia. But every Australian colony, however strong its aspirations to political independence, is influenced in what may be called its manners by the mother country. Australia began its political life with as close an approach to an aristocracy as a new country can make, in the existence of the " squatters," most of whom were capitalists or scions of good English families. These men obtained large grants of land from the government for sheep-farming, which in the beginning they managed with convicts whom they hired from the state, and whom they were permitted to flog in case of misbehavior. Their life, in short, was very nearly that of the old cotton-planter in the South, with the " patriarchal " element wanting.

The first work of the new democracy was to overthrow them, and take their large tracts of land away from them. But the democracy did not succeed, and has not succeeded, in preventing the formation of an upper class of the " English gentleman" type. This is what the successful Australian still strives to be. He does not become "a man of the people," in our sense, and does not boast of his humble origin and early struggles, as much as our millionaire is apt to do. The influence of this type was prolonged and strengthened by the large emigration to Australia of university graduates from England, during the fifties and sixties, after the colonies had fairly entered on free government, when a successful career at the bar and in public life had become possible. These, again, were reinforced by a still larger emigration of broken-down men of good family, who, if they added but little to the wealth or morality of the colonies, did a good deal to preserve the predominance of English conventional ideas. For instance, one of the very strong English traditions is the right of men of education and prominence to public offices; that is, men previously raised above the crowd by wealth or rank or education, or by some outward sign of distinction. This was perpetuated in the colonies by their connection with England in the way I have mentioned. It made the careers of such men as Robert Low and Gavan Duffy and Dr. Pensores, and many others, easy and natural, and made the breaking away from English ideas on social questions more difficult. Perhaps as important was the fact that it preserved the English way of living as the thing for the "self-made man" to aspire to. How strong this influence is in the Anglo-Saxon world may be inferred from the difficulty of keeping English influence in these matters in due subordination in this country. Nearly all our rich people, and people who have enjoyed any social success in England, are apt to revert to English life, and have to be ridiculed and denounced in the press in order to make them continue "good Americans."

In democracies which still look to England as "home," and which receive large bodies of immigrants educated in England, it can be easily understood how great must be the English influence on the colonial way of looking at both politics and society. In later days, when the democracy has fairly broken loose from the control of the Foreign Office, gifted men of the earlier American kind — that is, good speakers or writers — have in a large degree preserved their sway. The multiplicity of new questions, and the possibility of getting into power at any time by overthrowing the existing ministry, have naturally kept alive the art of discussion as the art which leads to political eminence. Thus far, undoubtedly, this has prevented the rise of any system like our caucus, which attaches little importance to speech or power of persuasion. In

Australia a man can hardly get high office without a general election. He has to produce a change of opinion in the legislature, or so great a change of opinion out of doors as to intimidate the legislature, either in order to see his policy adopted by the men actually in power, or to be charged himself with the formation of a new ministry. That is, the man most successful in exposition, who identifies himself by speech most prominently with some pending question, becomes, under the cabinet system, the man entitled to power, and no caucus nomination could either give it to him or deprive him of it. This more than aught else has made easy individual prominence by means of parliamentary arts. Of course, there is behind all talk a good deal of intrigue and chicanery, but talk there has to be. The cabinet system — or the possibility of changing majorities in the legislature at any time without waiting for a fixed term — makes it absolutely necessary that a successful politician should be able to express himself. He may be uneducated, in the technical sense of the term, but he must be master of his own subject, and be able to give a good account of it. He has to propose something energetically, in order to hold his place. Thus, Sir Charles Cowper and Robert Low had to connect themselves with the educational system, Sir Henry Parkes with the land system, and so on. The minister, whoever he is, is in constant danger of losing his place; the "outs" are constantly eager to displace him, and they displace him, as in England, by bringing up new questions, or new aspects of old ones.

The system, as I have already said, has the well-known defect of instability in the executive. It means in Australia, as it means in France and Italy, incessant change or frequent changes. It is what our founders dreaded when they put the President in office for four years, and Congress for two years, and made each independent of the other. But it has the effect of preventing the formation of strict party ties, controlled by a manager who has not to render any public account of his management. In other words, the caucus ruled by the boss is hardly possible under it. The boss is hardly possible, if he has to explain the reasons of his actions, and to say what he thinks the party policy ought to be. Whether this system would survive the formation of a confederacy like ours, and the necessity of more potent machinery to get a larger multitude to take part in elections, is something which may reasonably be doubted. In large democracies the future probably belongs to the presidential system, with its better arrangements for the formation and preservation of strong parties.

working under stricter discipline and with less discussion.

The cabinet system, however, has had one excellent effect: it compels every minister who appeals to the constituencies for power to state at length and with minuteness his claims on their support. He sets forth his views and plans with a fullness and an amount of argumentation which are never met with nowadays in our party platforms. He makes a real plea for confidence in him personally, and he issues his programme immediately before the election which is to decide his fate. His opponent, or rival, issues a counter one, and the two together place before the constituencies an explanation of the political situation such as our voters rarely get. Each not only explains and argues in defense of his programme, but makes promises, which if he succeeds he may be almost immediately called on to fulfill. These two documents are, in fact, much more business-like than anything which our political men lay before us. In our presidential system, no one in particular is responsible for legislation, and the Congress elected one year does not meet till the next. The effect of these two circumstances has given our party platform a vagueness and a sonorousness, a sort of detachment from actual affairs, which make it somewhat resemble a Pope's encyclical. It does not contain a legislative programme. There is, in fact, no person competent to make one, because no person, or set of persons, would be charged with fulfilling it. It is "the party" which the voter supports, and the party is a body too indeterminate to be held to any sort of accountability. The platform, therefore, confines itself to expressing views, instead of making promises. It reveals the hopes, the fears, the dislikes, and the admirations of the party rather than its intentions. It expresses sympathy with nationalities struggling for freedom, affection for workingmen and a strong desire that people who hire them shall pay them a "fair wage," detestation of various forms of wrong-doing on the part of their opponents, and denunciation of the mischiefs to the country which these opponents have wrought. But it gives little inkling of what the party will really do if it gets into power. If it does nothing at all, it cannot be called to account except in the same vague and indefinite way. Nobody in particular is responsible for its shortcomings, because all its members are responsible in the same degree.

Take as an illustration of my meaning what has occurred in this country with regard to the existing currency difficulties. Both the Republican and Democratic platforms have declared in favor of having a good currency, but the Demo-

cratic platform simply demanded the coinage of
silver at a certain ratio to gold, and ascribed a
long list of evils to the failure of the nation to
furnish such a coinage; it described these evils
in terms of philanthropy rather than of finance.
It did not offer any explanation, in detail, of the
way free coinage of silver at the sixteen to one
ratio, would work; how it would affect foreign
exchange, or domestic investments, or creditors,
or savings-banks. It simply recommended the
plan passionately, as a just and humane thing,
and treated its opponents as sharks and tyrants.
No business man could learn anything from it
as to the prospects of his ventures under a silver
régime. The Republican platform, on the other
hand, declared its desire that the various kinds
of United States currency (ten in number)
should be of equal value. But it abstained
from saying precisely in what manner this equality of value would be preserved, and what steps
would be taken for the purpose. In spite of
the fact that it was dealing with a business
matter, it made no proposal which a business
man could weigh or even understand. The
result was that although Congress met within
four months of the election, and the election
had turned on the currency question, nothing
whatever was said or done about it. No one
in Congress felt any particular responsibility

about it, or could be called to account for not
bringing it up or trying to settle it. Yet every
one could, or would, express cordial agreement
with the platform.

Under the Australian system things would
have gone differently. Mr. McKinley would
have issued an address to the electors, saying
distinctly that he stood for the gold standard,
setting forth the precise manner in which he
meant to deal with the various forms of United
States currency in case he were elected, and
promising to do it immediately on his election.
Mr. Bryan would have issued a counter mani-
festo, stating not simply his objections to the
gold standard, but the exact way in which he
meant to get rid of it, and the probable effect
of this action on trade and industry. Consequently, after the election, one or other of them
would have met a Parliament which would have
demanded of him immediate legislation ; and if
he had failed to produce it promptly, he would
have been denounced as a traitor or an incompetent, and a vote of want of confidence would
have turned him out of office. In short, the
winning man would have had to produce at once
something like the plan which our Monetary
Commission, composed of men not in political
life at all, has laboriously formed.

There occurred in Queensland, when Sir

George Bowen was governor, in 1867, a financial crisis which makes clear the difference between the Australian system and ours. The ministry had borrowed £1,000,000 sterling through a Sydney bank, to be spent in public works. The works had been begun, and £50,000 of the money had been received and a large number of men employed, when the bank failed. The ministers in office instantly proposed to issue " inconvertible government notes," like our greenbacks during the war, and make them legal tender in the colony. The governor informed them that he should have to veto such a bill, as his instructions required him to " reserve for the Queen's pleasure " every bill whereby any paper or other currency might be made a legal tender, " except the coin of the realm, or other gold or silver coin." But the ministers persisted. The populace of Brisbane were told by a few stump orators that " an issue of unlimited greenbacks would create unlimited funds for their employment on public works, while at the same time it would ruin the bankers, squatters [great sheep-farmers], and other capitalists," whom the people hated. A so-called indignation meeting was held, at which the governor and a majority of the legislature were denounced in violent terms ; several leading members of Parliament were ill-treated in the streets, and threats were even uttered of burning down Government House.[1]

The governor held firm, and insisted on meeting the crisis by the issue of exchequer bills; so the ministry resigned, and was succeeded by another, which did issue the exchequer bills. Had the governor not held his ground, the colony would have been launched on a sea of irredeemable paper, from which escape would probably have been difficult. In fact, there is little doubt that it is the necessity of making their loans in England, and thus getting the approval of British capitalists for their financial expedients, which has saved the colonies from even worse excesses in currency matters. The immediate responsibility of the minister for legislation must make all crises short, if sharp. No abnormal financial situation in any of the Australian colonies could last as long as ours has done, and while they retain their connection with the British crown they will be preserved from the very tempting device of irredeemable paper.

An effort has been made in some of the colonies to get rid of changefulness in the executive by electing the ministers by popular suffrage, instead of having them elected by Parliament; but this attempt to depart from the cabinet sys-

[1] *Thirty Years of Colonial Government.* From the Official Papers of Sir G. F. Bowen.

tem has apparently been made only by the
" labor party," or workingman's party, which
exists and grows, without having as yet been
successful in getting hold of office. Its main
strength seems to lie, as in this country, in influence ; that is, in alarming members of Parliament about its vote. It hangs over the heads of
the legislators *in terrorem*, in closely divided
constituencies, but does not often make its way
into Parliament itself, though those of its members who have been elected seem to acquit themselves very creditably.

The first strong resemblance between our
experience and that of the Australians is to be
found in the educational system. The first
attempts at popular education, as might have
been expected, were made by the clergy of the
Anglican Church, the only church which had
official recognition in the early days of the colonies. All money voted by the government for
this purpose was given to the clergy and dis-
tributed by them. The instruction was mainly
religious, and the catechism and reading of the
Scriptures in the Protestant version played a
prominent part in it. From the beginning, the
opposition to this, on the part of all the other
denominations, was very strong. As in America,
the opposition of the Catholics was not directed
against denominational teaching. They were

willing to have the state money equally divided
among the clergy, so that each denomination
might control the instruction given to its own
children. To this plan all the other denominations, except the Anglicans, were violently hostile; so that on this question the Protestant
Episcopalians and the Catholics were united.
Their clergy wanted the state money for their
own kind of education, while those of other
denominations were in favor of secular education, or common schools, paid for largely by the
state, though not wholly, as here.

It would be tedious to go over the history of
the struggle which resulted in the establishment
of state schools, with secular teaching. It bore
a close resemblance to our own struggle, but differed in having for the efforts of the Protestant
Episcopalians powerful support from the home
government, which then, as now, sympathized
with denominational teaching. It ended, finally,
in the triumph of the secular schools. Secular
education seems to be the established democratic
method of teaching the young, though the desire of the clergy to keep control of education
is giving it an anti-religious trend in some countries, — France, for instance. The agitation of
this subject in Australia has brought out the
interesting fact that the Catholic population,
almost wholly Irish and very large, sides with

the priests on nearly every public question, the
educational question among others. This is
exactly what has occurred in England. In the
late conflict over the schools in England, the
Irish voted with the Tories in favor of denominational teaching. Like most national oddities,
there is for this an historical explanation. The
banishment of the old Irish gentry, beginning
in Elizabeth's time, and ending with the Revolution of 1688, deprived the Irish of their natural political leaders. The new gentry were foreigners in race and religion, and in political
sympathies. This threw the people back on the
priests, who became their only advisers possessing
any education or knowledge of the world, and
assumed without difficulty a political leadership
which has never been shaken to this day, in spite
of the growing activity of the lay element in Irish
politics. No Irish layman has, as yet, proved a
very successful politician, in the long run, who
has not managed to keep the clergy at his back.

It may be said that, on the whole, the educational movement in Australia has been controlled
by influences common to the rest of the civilized world. In nearly all countries there is a
struggle going on — which ended with us many
years ago — to wrest the control of the popular
schools, wherever they exist, from the hands of
the clergy, who have held it for twelve hundred

years. No characteristic of the old régime in politics is more prominent than the belief that the priests or ministers only should have charge of the training of youth. Almost the whole history of the educational movement in this century is the history of the efforts of the " Liberals" or " Radicals " to oust them.

The Australians resemble us also in having an immense tract of land at the disposition of the state. They came into possession much later, when waste lands were more accessible, before they were covered by traditions of any sort, and when the air had become charged with the spirit of experimentation. They have accordingly tried to do various things with the land, which we never thought of. South Australia, for instance, had the plan of giving grants of land to small coöperative associations, to be managed by trustees, and supplied with capital by a loan from the state of not more than $250 a head. The state, in short, agreed to do what our Populists think it ought to do, — lend money to the farmers at a low rate of interest. Some of these associations were plainly communistic, and the members were often brought together simply by poverty. As a whole, they have not succeeded. Some have broken up; others remain and pay the government its interest, but no one expects that it will ever get back the principal.

In New South Wales, the state became a land-
lord on an extensive scale on the Henry George
plan, and the question of rents then grew into a
great political question. Political "pressure"
is brought to bear on the fixing of the rents, and
the management, of course, gives a very large
field for "pulls" and "influence." In Queensland, which has a tropical sugar region, not only
have lands been rented by the state, but cheap
carriage has been provided for farm and dairy
produce on the state railway, bonuses have been
paid on the export of dairy produce, advances
have been made to the proprietors of works for
freezing meat, and it has been proposed to establish state depots in London for the receipt and
distribution of frozen meat. One act makes provision, under certain conditions, for a state guar-
antee for loans contracted to build sugar-works.
In New Zealand, there is a graduated tax intended to crush out large landholders; but any
landholder who is dissatisfied with his assessment
can require the government to purchase at its
own valuation, and land is rented in small holdings. The government has also borrowed large
sums of money to lend to farmers on mortgage.
It sends lecturers on butter-making and fruit-
growing around the country. It pays wages to
labor associations who choose to settle on state
lands and clear or improve them, and then allows

them to take up the holdings thus improved. It keeps a " state farm," on which it gives work to the unemployed. All these things, of course, give it a great number of favors to bestow or withhold, and open a wide field for political intrigue.

As a general rule, the suffrage is adult and male, but there is a property qualification for voters for the upper houses of the legislatures, answering to our Senates. Members of both houses are paid a small salary. At first they all served voluntarily, as in England, and the payment of members was not brought about without a good deal of agitation. But the argument which carried the day for payment was, not, as might be supposed, the justice of giving poor men a chance of seats, but the necessity, in a busy community, of securing for the work of government the services of many competent men who could not afford to give their time without pay. The " plum " idea of a seat in the legislature can hardly be said to have made its appearance yet. The necessity of doing something for " labor " very soon became prominent in colonial policy, and one of its first triumphs was the contraction of very large loans in England for the construction of public works, mainly railroads and common roads, the creation of village settlements and the advance of money to them. The result of all this, after a while, was tremendous financial collapse, and the discharge of large bodies of the very laborers for whose benefit the works were undertaken. This calamity seems to have stimulated the tendency to tax the rich heavily, and to foster the policy of protection. Trade is promoted not simply by duties on imports, but by state aid to exports. A depot in London, which does not pay its own expenses, takes charge of Australian goods and guarantees their quality; bonuses are given to particular classes of producers, and there is even talk of a " produce export department" of the government. The protectionist policy has taken possession of the Australian mind even more firmly than it has taken possession of the mind of the Republican party here. A free-trader comes nearer being looked upon as a " crank " in most of the colonies than he does here. But the " infant industry" there has solid claims to nurture which it does not possess in this country. In fact, the dominance of the protectionist theory is so strong that it forms one of the obstacles in the promotion of the proposed Australian confederation, as no colony is quite willing to give up its right to tax imports from all the others, and still less is it willing to join Mr. Chamberlain's followers and let in free the goods of the mother country. We may conjecture from this what obstacles the policy of free internal trade between our states would have met with at the foundation of our government, had America been more of a manufacturing community, and had intercommunication been easier. The difficulty of carriage a hundred years ago formed a natural tariff, which made the competition of foreigners seem comparatively unimportant.

From the bestowal of responsible government in the fifties, down to 1893, nearly all the colonies reveled in the ease with which they could borrow money in England. There was a great rush to make state railroads, in order to open up the lands of the great landholders to projects favored by labor, and to give employment to workingmen; and, after the railroads were made, they carried workingmen for next to nothing. Along with this came an enormous development of the civil service, somewhat like our increase of pensions. New South Wales alone had 200,000 persons in government offices, at a salary of $13,000,000, and 10,000 railroad employees to boot. This gave the ministries for the time being great influence, which was increased by the fact that the state was the owner of large tracts of land, which it rented on favorable terms to favored tenants. The excitement of apparent prosperity, too, brought into the legislature large numbers of men to whom salary was important, and the result was perhaps the first serious decline in the character of the Australian governments. The colonies were founded between 1788 and 1855. Up to this time they have spent $800,000,000 on public works. They have made 80,000 miles of telegraph, and 10,000 miles of railway. Though they have a revenue of only $117,500,000, they have already a debt of $875,000,000.

These "good times" came to their natural end. By 1893 the money was all spent, the taxation was not sufficient to meet the interest, the English capitalists refused further advances, the banks failed on all sides, and the colonies were left with large numbers of unemployed on their hands. There was nothing for it but to spend more money on "relief works," and to keep almost permanently in the employment of the state large bodies of men, who liked it simply because it was easy, and because hard times were a sufficient excuse for seeking it. What one learns from the experience of the colonies in the matter of expenditure is the difficulty, in a democratic government, of moderation of any description, if it once abandons the policy of *laissez faire*, and undertakes to be a providence for the masses. There is no limit to the human appetite for unearned or easily earned money. No class is exempt from it. Under the old régime, the aristocrats got all the sinecures, the pensions, and the light jobs of every description. One of the results of the triumph of democracy has been to throw open this source of gratification to the multitude, and every attempt made to satisfy the multitude, in this field, has failed. When the French opened the national workshops in Paris in 1848, the government speedily found that it was likely to have the whole working class of Paris on its hands; when we started our pension list, we found that peace soon became nearly as expensive as war; and when the Australians undertook to develop the country on money borrowed by the state, there was no restraint on their expenditure, except the inability to find any more lenders. The Australian financial crisis was brought about, not by any popular perception that the day of reckoning was at hand, but by the refusal of the British capitalists to make further loans.

It is in devices for the protection of labor that most of this experimentation occurs. New Zealand affords the best example of it. It provides elaborate legal protection for the eight-hour day. A workman cannot consent to work overtime without extra pay. The state sees that he gets the extra pay. It looks closely after the condition of women and children in the factories. It sees that servant girls are not overcharged by the registry offices for getting them places. It prescribes one half-holiday a week for all persons employed in stores and offices, and sees that they take it. It will not allow even a shopkeeper who has no employees to dispense with his half-holiday; because if he does not take it, his competition will injure those who do. The "labor department" of the government has an army of inspectors, who keep a close watch on stores and factories, and prosecute violations of the law which they themselves discover. They do not wait for complaints; they ferret out infractions, so that the laborer may not have to prejudice himself by making charges. The department publishes a "journal" once a month, which gives detailed reports of the condition of the labor market in all parts of the colony, and of the prosecutions which have taken place anywhere of employers who have violated the law. It provides insurance for old age and early death, and guarantees every policy. It gives larger policies for lower premiums than any of the private offices, and depreciates the private offices in its documents. It distributes the profits of its business as bonuses among the policy holders, and keeps a separate account for teetotalers, so that they may get special advantages from their abstinence. The "journal" is, in fact, in a certain sense a labor manual, in which everything pertaining to the comfort of labor is freely discussed. The poor accommodation provided for servants in hotels and restaurants is deplored, and so is the difficulty which middle-aged men have in finding employment. More attention to the morals and manners of nursemaids is recommended. All the little dodges of employers are exposed and punished. If they keep the factory door fastened, they are fined. If housekeepers pretend that their servants are lodgers, and therefore not liable to a compulsory half-holiday, they are fined. If manufacturers are caught allowing girls to take their meals in a workshop, they are fined.

As far as I can make out, too, without visiting the country, there is as yet no sign of reaction against this minute paternal care of the laborer. The tendency to use the powers of the government chiefly for the promotion of the comfort of the working classes, whether in the matter of land settlement, education, or employment, seems to undergo no diminution. The only thing which has ceased or slackened is the borrowing of money for improvements. The results of this borrowing have been so disastrous that the present generation, at least, will hardly try that experiment again. Every new country possessing a great body of undeveloped resources, like those of the North American continent and

of Australia, must rely largely on foreign capital
for the working of its mines and the making of
its railroads. In this country all that work has
been left to private enterprise, or, in other words,
to the activity of individuals and corporations.
Apart from some recent land-grants to railroads
and the sale of public lands at low rates, it may
be said that our government has done nothing
whatever to promote the growth of the national
wealth and population. The battle with nature,
on this continent, has been fought mainly by
individuals. The state, in America, has con-
tented itself, from the earliest times, with supplying education and security. Down to a very
recent period the American was distinguished
from the men of all other countries, for looking
to the government for nothing but protection
to life and property. Tocqueville remarked
strongly on this, when he visited the United
States in the thirties. This habit has been a
good deal broken up by the growth of the wage-
earning class since the war, by the greatly increased reliance on the tariff, and by the government issue of paper money during the
rebellion. In the eyes of many, these things
have worked a change in the national character.
But we are still a great distance from the Australian policy. The development of the country
by the state, in the Australian sense, has only

recently entered into the heads of our labor and socialist agitators. The American plan has hitherto been to facilitate private activity, to make rising in the world easy for the energetic individual, and to load him with praise and influence after he has risen. This policy has been pursued so far that, in the opinion of many, the individual has become too powerful, and the government too subservient to private interests. There are in fact few, if any, states in the Union which are not said to be dominated by rich men or rich corporations.

This is a not unnatural result of two things. One is, as I have said, our having left the development of the country almost wholly to private enterprises. It is individual capitalists who have worked the mines, made the railroads, invited the immigrants, and lent them money to improve their farms. The other is the restrictions which the state constitutions, and the courts construing them, place on the use of the taxes. There are very few things the state in America can constitutionally do with its revenue, compared with what European governments can do. Aids to education are tolerated, because education is supposed to equip men more thoroughly for the battle of life, but the American public shrinks from any other use of the public funds for private benefit. We give little or no help to art, or literature, or charity, or hospitals. We lend no money. We issued legal tender paper under many protests and in a time of great national trial, have never ceased to regret it, and shall probably never do it again. We are angry when we find that any one enjoys comforts or luxury at the expense of the state. We cannot bear sinecures. But our plunge into pensions since the war shows that there now exists among us the same strong tendency to get things out of the state, and to rely on its bounty, which prevails in Australia. It is difficult to resist the conclusion that at present we owe a good deal of what remains of *laissez faire* in our policy to our constitutions and courts. We owe the constitutions and the courts to the habits formed in an earlier stage of American history. It was the bad or good fortune of the Australian colonies to enter on political life just as the let-alone policy was declining under the influence of the humanitarian feeling which the rise of the democracy has brought with it everywhere. More constitution than was supplied by the enabling acts of the British Parliament was never thought of, and the British Parliament did not think of imposing any restraints on legislation except those which long custom or British opinion imposed on Parliament itself.

The result is that Australia is absolutely free

to democratic experimentation under extremely favorable circumstances. In each colony the state has apparently existed for the benefit of the working classes, who must always constitute the majority of the people in every community, and the masses have been provided with work and protection, in complete disregard of European traditions. The experiment has turned out pretty well, owing to the abundance of land, the natural wealth of the country, and the fineness of the climate. But each colony is forming its political habits, and I cannot resist the conclusion that some of them are habits which are likely to plague the originators hereafter. For instance, the task of finding work for the unemployed, and borrowing money for the purpose, though this generation has seen it fail utterly in the first trial, will probably be resorted to again, with no more fortunate results. Nor can I believe that the growing paternalism, the sedulous care of the business interests of the masses, will not end by diminishing self-reliance, and increasing dependence on the state.

The worst effects of these two agencies, of course, in a country of such wonderful resources as Australia, must be long postponed. There are hindrances to progress in the direction of pure " collectivism " yet in existence, many problems to be solved, Old World influences to be got rid of, before Australia finds herself perfectly free from the trammels which the régime of competition still throws around every modern society. But so far as I can judge from the accounts of even the most impartial observers, every tendency which is causing us anxiety or alarm here is at work there, without any hindrance from constitutions ; though there is great comfort among the people, and there is a hopefulness which cannot but exist in any new country with immense areas of vacant land and a rapidly growing population.

One check to all leveling tendencies is the extremely strong hold which the competitive system has taken of the Anglo-Saxon race. There is no other race in which there is still so much of the rude energy of the earlier world, in which men have such joy in rivalry and find it so hard to surrender personal advantages. This renders communal life of any kind, or any species of enforced equality, exceedingly difficult. It will probably endanger the permanence of all the social experimentation in Australia, as soon as this experimentation plainly gives evidence of bestowing special advantages on the weak, or lazy, or unenterprising. There is not in Australia the same extravagant admiration of wealth as a sign of success that there is here, but there are signs of its coming. The state has under-

taken to do so many things, however, through
which individuals make fortunes here, that its
coming may be slow. The wealthy Australian,
who dislikes rude colonial ways, and prefers to
live in England, is already a prominent figure in
London society, and, like the rich Europeanized
American, he is an object of great reprobation
to the plain Australian, who has not yet " made
his pile " and cannot go abroad. Then there is
a steady growth of national pride, which is dis-
playing itself in all sorts of ways, — in literature, art, and above all athletics, as well as in
trade and commerce. The development of ath-
letic and sporting tastes generally is greater
than elsewhere, and competition is the life of
athletics. An athlete is of little account until
he has beaten somebody in something. " The
record " is the record of superiority of somebody
in something over other people. The " duffer "
is the man who can never win anything. The
climate helps to foster these tastes, and the
abundance of everything makes the cultivation
of them easy ; but they are tastes which must
always make the sinking of superiority — or, in
other words, any communal system — difficult.
Australia may develop a higher type of character or better equipment for the battle of life,
and more numerous opportunities, but it is
hardly likely to develop any new form of society.

When the struggle grows keener, we are not likely to see a corresponding growth of state aid.

The very rapidity of the experimentation now going on promises to bring about illuminating crises earlier there than here. Probably we shall not get our currency experience here for many years to come. Were the Australians engaged in trying our problem, they would reach a solution in one or two years. We are likely in the next hundred years to see a great many new social ventures tried, something which the wreck of authority makes almost inevitable ; but there seems no reason to believe that the desire of the Anglo-Saxon variety of human nature to profit by superiority in any quality will disappear. The cabinet system of government is in itself a strong support to individuality, for reasons I have already given.

Another steadying influence in Australia, perhaps one of the most powerful in a democratic community, is the press. The press, from all I can learn, is still serious, able, and influential. It gives very large space to athletics and similar amusements, but seems to have retained a high and potent position in the discussions of the day. The love of triviality which has descended on the American press like a flood, since the war, has apparently passed by that of Australia. Why

this should be, I confess I have not been able
to discover, and can hardly conjecture. If we
judge by what has happened in America, it
would be easy to conclude that the press in all
democracies is sure to become somewhat puerile,
easily occupied with small things, and prone to
flippant treatment of great subjects. This is
true of the French press, in a way; but in that
case something of the tendency may be ascribed
to temperament, and something to want of practice in self-government. I cannot see any signs
of it in the country press in England. That,
so far as I have been able to observe, continues
grave, decorous, and mature. There is nothing
of the boyish spirit in it which pervades much of
our journalism. The weight which still attaches
to the tastes and opinions of an educated upper
class may account for this in some degree, but
the fact is that Australian journals have preserved these very characteristics, although the
beginnings of Australian journalism were as bad
as possible. Its earliest editing was done by ex-
convicts, and the journals which these men set
on foot were very like those that have the worst
reputation among us for venality and triviality.
Strange to say, the community did not sit down
under them. There was an immediate rising
against this sort of editors in New South Wales.
Their control of leading newspapers was treated

as a scandal too great to be borne, and they were driven out of the profession. The newspapers then passed largely into the hands of young university men who had come out from England to seek their fortunes; they gave journalism a tone which has lasted till now. The opinions of the press still count in politics. It can still discredit or overthrow a ministry, because the duration of a ministry depends on the opinion of the legislature, and that, in turn, depends on the opinion of the public. There can be no defiant boss, indifferent to what the public thinks, provided he has "got the delegates." In fact, the Australian system seems better adapted to the maintenance of really independent and influential journals than ours. The fixed terms of executive officers and the boss system of nomination are almost fatal to newspaper power. So long as results cannot be achieved quickly, the influence of the press must be feeble.

Of course, in speaking of a country which one does not know personally, one must speak very cautiously. All impressions one gets from books need correction by actual observation, particularly in the case of a country in which changes are so rapid as in Australia. Of this rapidity every traveler and writer I have consulted makes mention, and every traveler soon finds his book out of date. Sir Charles Dilke visited Australia about 1870, but writing in 1890 he dwells on the enormous differences of every kind which twenty years had brought about. The latest work on Australia, Mr. Walker's "Australasian Democracy," gives as an illustration of this transientness of everything the fact that the three colonies of New South Wales, South Australia, and Victoria have had respectively twenty-eight, forty-two, and twenty-six ministries in forty years. One can readily imagine how many changes of policy on all sorts of subjects, and how many changes of men, these figures represent. All travelers, too, bear testimony to the optimism of the people in every colony. Nothing is more depressing in a new country than officialism, or management of public affairs by irresponsible rulers. From this the Anglo-Saxons have always enjoyed freedom in their new countries. The result has always been free play for individual energy and initiative; and with boundless resources, as in America and Australia, these qualities are sure to bring cheerfulness of temperament. The mass of men are better off each year, mistakes are not serious, mutual helpfulness is the leading note of the community, nobody is looked down on by anybody, and public opinion is all powerful. In Australia there is more reason for this, as yet, than with us. The Australians are not tormented by a race question, they have never had any civil strife, and they have not yet come into contact with that greatest difficulty of large democracies, the difficulty of communicating to the mass common ideas and impulses.

NOTE.   As I have endeavored to give in this chapter impressions rather than facts, I have not thought it worth while to cite authorities for all my statements.   I will simply say that I have formed these impressions from the perusal of the following works : The Australian Colonies in 1896, E. A. Petherick, 1897 ; New Zealand Rulers and Statesmen, 1840–97, William Gisborne ; Oceana, J. A. Froude, 1886 ; Queensland, Rev. John D. Lang, D. D., 1864 ; The Coming Commonwealth, R. R. Garlan, 1897 ; The Australians, Francis Adams, 1893 ; The Land of Gold, Julius M. Price, 1896 ; New Zealand Official Year Book, 1897 ; Reports of Department of Labor, 1893–97 ; Journal of 1897; Problems of Greater Britain, Sir Charles Dilke, 1890 ; Historical and Statistical Account of New South Wales, Dr. Lang, 1875 ; Thirty Years of Colonial Government, Sir G. F. Bowen, 1889 ; Australian Democracy, Henry de R. Walker, 1897 ; History of New Zealand, G. W. Rusden, 1891 ; Western Australian Blue Book.